THE OTHER SIDE OF THE STORY

Daphine Priscilla Brown-Jack

Edited and formatted by Leah Chase from LC Editing Services. Contact at lcg.chase@gmail.com

Scripture taken from the King James Version of the Bible.

ISBN: 13-9784-7200-4946-3

Psalm 31

The Heart of Psalms' Music Director Speaks to and for the Hearts of the Involved Musicians

In you, Lord, I have taken refuge;

let me never be put to shame;

deliver me in your righteousness.

Turn your ear to me,

come quickly to my rescue;

be my rock of refuge,

a strong fortress to save me.

Since you are my rock and my fortress,

for the sake of your name lead and guide me.

Keep me free from the trap that is set for me,

for you are my refuge.

Into your hands I commit my spirit;

deliver me, Lord, my faithful God.

I hate those who cling to worthless idols;

as for me, I trust in the Lord.

I will be glad and rejoice in your love,

for you saw my affliction

and knew the anguish of my soul.

You have not given me into the hands of the enemy

but have set my feet in a spacious place.

Be merciful to me, Lord, for I am in distress;

my eyes grow weak with sorrow,

my soul and body with grief.

My life is consumed by anguish

and my years by groaning;

my strength fails because of my affliction, [b]

and my bones grow weak

Because of all my enemies,

I am the utter contempt of my neighbors

and an object of dread to my closest friends —

those who see me on the street flee from me.

I am forgotten as though I were dead;

I have become like broken pottery.

For I hear many whispering,

"Terror on every side!"

They conspire against me

and plot to take my life.

But I trust in you, Lord;

I say, "You are my God."

My times are in your hands;

deliver me from the hands of my enemies,

from those who pursue me.

Let your face shine on your servant;

save me in your unfailing love.

Let me not be put to shame, Lord,

for I have cried out to you;

but let the wicked be put to shame

and be silent in the realm of the dead.

Let their lying lips be silenced,

for with pride and contempt

they speak arrogantly against the righteous.

19 How abundant are the good things

that you have stored up for those who fear you,

that you bestow in the sight of all,

on those who take refuge in you.

In the shelter of your presence you hide them

from all human intrigues;

you keep them safe in your dwelling

from accusing tongues.

Praise be to the Lord,

for he showed me the wonders of his love

when I was in a city under siege.

In my alarm I said,

"I am cut off from your sight!"

Yet you heard my cry for mercy

when I called to you for help.

Love the Lord, all his faithful people!

The Lord preserves those who are true to him,

but the proud he pays back in full.

Be strong and take heart,

all you who hope in the Lord.

To my sweet ladies,

Daphine, Mary, and Katherine

Contents

YEAR 2012

YEAR 2013

Acknowledgements

I would like to thank God for this opportunity to express myself in writing. It has been a long journey toward making a decision to write this book. I would like to thank my husband, my two daughters, and my son for helping me complete this book as well as for putting up with my emotional roller coaster. I would like to thank my amazing editorial team who unselfishly came together and gave their professional expertise and time to make this book a success: Connie LeDay, Janet Gipson, Cynthia Warren, and author Lily Parker. I appreciate the publishing company for encouraging me to continue writing. I thank God for my dad and my mother and for their raising me to be honest. I would like to thank my close, resourceful friends who walked me through the process. Special thanks to the following people: Pastor William and Sister Sharon Hennesey (True Vine COGIC); Bishop and Sister H. Richardson Sr.; Elder and Sister C. Turner; Dr. Gladys Lockett-Ross; Mother Doris Carter; Veronica Jolivette; Elder T. Leon Preston and Marie Preston; my sweet cousin Pastor Ivan and my sweet Cassandra Gordon; the Jack family; the late Ms. Maudi Linton Brown; Uncle Joe and the late Aunt Ruth; my cousins from Malmedy Street, Toby Brown, Pastor Clenton Brown, Evangelist Pearline Matson, and Joyce Brown; Marla Wolsky; attorneys Lyn Shepherd, Jimmy Brown, Stanley Ray Mays, Natasha Thompson, Andrew McGee, Chi Roberson, and Bryan Garris; Professor J. W. Stanley; Ariana de Valdivia; Felicia Dye-Parker, owner of Salon of a Lifetime; Debbie Porter Photography; Gwen Walter; all the therapists who kept my family together; my sweet neighbors who encouraged my family; Jason "J. Shep" Shepherd for writing "Haven't Forgot," a song letting us know that God hasn't forgotten us; and Al Reese, Lakeshia Reese Sessum, Rev. Dr. Barbara L. Williams, Raquel Williams, Chantel Moon, and Triston Batts.

Foreword

The Other Side of the Story is a heartfelt invitation from Mrs. Jack. The reader is invited to accompany the author on her journey through the stormy seasons of her life.

Acceptance of the invitation leads the reader over potholes, around curves, and beyond detours in the family's travels. We wait for the drama to unfold. However, we observe the internalizing of broken spirits and bruised aspirations. Changes in the landscape of this family are presented with incredible candor and spirituality.

Mrs. Jack addresses critical components of life from her perspective. Her side of the story is proclaimed in a nonjudgmental, faltering, and evolving voice. As the core of the family's authenticity is assailed, the imagery of her oasis emerges. There are friends extending the balm of kindness, loyalty, and encouragement.

This is not a testimony of a superwoman but a woman with human weaknesses and a super faith. She refuses to allow the darkness of humiliation to infect her entire life. Her spirit is illuminated. The writer liberally shares nuggets on the workings of the justice system, which can be beneficial when we least expect it.

From the first flash of lightning during the storm to the appearance of their rainbow, she strives to preserve the harmony of her family. She questions and falters while focusing soul and mind on the source of her strength, God.

This is not a work of coercion but of conviction. It is not presented as the way through storms but her way through her storms.

Readers, we are candidates for letting disillusions, unfairness, and temptations of anger and bitterness appear in our lives. This side of the story challenges us to embrace it all with a new song.

The family is applauded as they transition from peril to a place of peace.

Lily Parker, author
Nostalgia Bittersweet
State of the Heart
Go Tell Michele (contributor)

Preface

This book is about the emotional torment my family and I experienced while going through an unimaginable situation with my husband, who was falsely accused. I share how I dealt with this emotional burden for five years. I was at the brink of self destruction, but with faith and my trust in God, I began to realize that God would bring me through, no matter what the outcome was.

This book also tells about the financial difficulties caused by the unfairness of the criminal justice system. It will encourage you to fight and not give into a plea bargaining system that is set up to make you fail if you have not committed a crime.

The story is written in chronological order from 2009 until it ends in 2013. I have changed the names of some of the people.

The reason I chose a black book cover is that I wanted to represent the darkness of the mind when dealing with the justice system. The man standing in the doorway represents my husband. In this image, he is unable to know what is on the other side of the door, but is just standing for truth, leaving the scales of justice behind.

The book will encourage you to stand for the truth and trust in God!

Introduction

After an hour and a half, the jury returned with the verdict. My heart began to pump cold blood through my veins as anxiety overwhelmed me. I wanted to go into the courtroom and hear the verdict, but fear grasped me and weakened my innermost being, the part that kept me sane. My body began to weaken like a flower deprived of water. Given the sick feeling in my gut, it was to my advantage that the investigator had me go sit in the waiting room. It was almost as if she felt my pulse racing—as if she could read my mind.

While my son, daughters, and I waited for the verdict, we prayed. As we sat in dead silence, I noticed the uneasiness of my youngest daughter. I could not quite read her true feelings, but I knew something was wrong. As I observed her, she stood and then bolted out of the room. Concerned, I asked the investigator to go find her and check on her. When the investigator came back, she informed me that she was fine. The investigator then went to sit in the courtroom to hear the verdict. I sat at the edge of my seat while my eldest daughter cried, "I know it is not guilty! I know it is not guilty." A few minutes later, I noticed the doorknob turning, and my heart began to beat like never before.

The investigator opened the door.

Chapter 1

The Story of Job

Have you ever encountered events in your life that were devastating and seemed to never end? Or just one event where you almost lost your mind? And not only did you almost lose your mind, but you also almost lost, or did lose, your material possessions and close friends or family members, experienced a change in your relationships, or spent your entire life savings? For some reason, though, you still remained faithful to God, and because of your faithfulness, you were able to regroup, recover, and rebuild.

Some of you might be still going through such an event, but think about the story of Job. He lost his material possessions and his sons and daughters. He even became ill, and his wife said, "Curse God and die!" But Job recovered because of his faithfulness to God.

Job's faith was tested, and he passed the test by remaining faithful. Our faith is also tested. The question is, can we pass the test? As human beings, it is natural for us to become weak in a moment of despair. We can't think straight or even ask God why something is happening.

Each one of us has a test prepared specifically for us, and each one of us will pass through the test in a different way I can stand your test, and you can't stand mine.

The saying "God won't give you more than you can bear" derives from 1 Corinthians 10:13: "There hath no temptation taken you but such as is common to man: but God is faithful, who will not suffer you to be tempted above that ye are able; but will with the temptation also make a way to escape, that ye may be able to bear it" (KJV).

When you trust and believe in God, the situation does come to an end. I am telling you something I know and have experienced. Here is my story.

2009

Chapter 2

Academics and Life Education

In August, my husband and I traveled about six hundred miles to drop off my oldest daughter at college. I had mixed feelings about leaving my firstborn in a small town far away from home.

After we arrived, we helped her unpack and settle into her dorm. We then said farewell without any emotion. As we drove off to travel back home, it hit me that I had just left a wonderful young lady to begin her life. She was not my baby anymore. The tears began to flow, but I didn't want my husband to see me crying.

Just as I was about to really start wailing, my phone rang. It was my daughter. "Mama, I forgot my phone charger in the car." That ended my outburst of tears. We turned around and dropped off her phone charger. I knew that God wanted me to drive off this time happy and not sad. Life can be so funny.

On August 26, everything was fine—at least I thought so. God had blessed my youngest daughter with getting into the middle school of her choice. While driving home from work, I began to reflect on my day. I was excited and thankful for my blessings. But then an unusual thought came to my mind: *today is too perfect.* I had a gut instinct that something was wrong.

My phone rang. It was my youngest daughter with some unbelievable news about a shameful allegation against my husband that didn't fit his character. A thought occurred in the back of my mind that I could be true, but after processing the elements of the allegation, none of it made any sense.

This allegation turned my life into turmoil. Everything began to fall apart. I felt defeated. Or was it a test of my faith? I didn't understand. I was doing everything I was supposed to do to make sure everyone was happy, and I was living the American dream: get married, have children, own your own home, and then retire. I was not selfish about spreading my love and peace to everyone.

A few hours later, I was mentally drained from trying to think this situation through. I had no desire to pray. I felt my faith weakening. I just wanted everything fixed now — right now — and back to normal. I remembered the storm in 2008 that had hit our home, but I didn't think another storm was about to hit my life.

I called Mary Louise, a very dear friend of my mom's who was like a mom to me. She was very dear to my family too. She said, "Girl, nothing happened. It is just the Devil stirring up a mess." She started to pray, and I started feeling a bit better. I just could not get past my life being interrupted with this stuff.

On September 29, things turned for the worse. I had to make some major decisions, as now more details were added to the shameful allegations against my husband.

On October 5, the situation grew to an immeasurable level. Our family had to split when the state forced my husband to move out of our home. Thus, began my education as a single parent. And now the state was a part of my life.

Truth was now my goal. In my inner sanctuary, my spirit revealed a truth. As I reflected on the nineteen years my husband and I had been married, I thought about the man I knew, the father of my children, and how important life was to him.

I was not going to choose sides. I needed to remain neutral, but I could no longer depend on anyone. It was now only God and me.

Late in the evening October 26, a second loss occurred in my life, this time a permanent one. My mother-in-law passed away. We don't always understand why things happen, but they are part of God's plan.

I received my answer from God about why my husband was forced to move out of our home. He had the opportunity to be with his mother during the last stage of her life. Although the state pulled our family apart, it wasn't a defeat because God knew the night He would take my mother-in-law to heaven.

Her death tore me into a million pieces. After a while, I knew I needed to pull myself together, but my mind was in too many places at once. I did not know where to start. The situation was impossible. I still had to investigate the allegations. How was I going to tell the children that their grandmother was deceased?

Two days later, a third loss occurred. Child Protective Services (CPS) came and took our two children. They said I wasn't protecting them from their father, so I was no longer allowed to be with them now, and it was possible I never would be again.

I called our attorney to ask him why my children were being taken. He said he didn't know and asked me what I had done wrong. I told him, "I did nothing wrong. We were just here at home, and the kids were doing their homework." After hanging up, I could no longer think straight.

It was a tragedy, but I could not find the tears while my children were being rushed out of our home. I had to get their medications together. They were allowed to take only the clothes they had on their backs, and I could not even give them a kiss or a hug good-bye.

The police officer who was assisting the caseworker called another police officer to assist with taking my kids from our home. I watched in disbelief as my children were driven away with the caseworker, thinking that this had to be a nightmare and wishing I could just wake up. But it was not a nightmare; it was real.

The police officer asked if I knew why the children were being taken. "No," I told her. "I did everything they asked me to do, but they took my children anyway." The police officer gave me a case number in case I needed to make a report.

After the kids were gone, I called Jenny to come and sit with me. Jenny was a coworker who had become like a real sister to me in a short time. She was there for me when I had no one else — someone I could say I truly depended on during this major storm in my life.

While I waited for her arrival, I called Mary Louise to tell her what had happened. She could not believe it and began to cry. "This has gone too far," she said. "Something has to be done to get this stuff resolved."

After hanging up, I began reading the documentation that gave the reason why CPS had picked up my children. I then called my attorney and read the documents to him.

He immediately said, "That is not true." I could tell by his tone that he was very angry. He said he and I would go to the courthouse the next morning to talk with the judge to find out why the children were taken. He ended by saying, "We have to keep praying."

I still couldn't cry. I was in disbelief that my children were gone. I wanted to call my husband and my oldest daughter to tell them what had happened, but I needed

daughter to tell them what had happened, but I needed to wait because I did not want to upset them. There was enough going on. I kept it to myself with an emptiness that was unemotionally unbearable. I just wanted to take my last breath.

Jenny arrived at my house, and I handed her the documents to read. "This does not make any sense," she said. I told her I had never heard of these allegations and that the information was not true. They took my children because of lies and inconsistent stories. I told Jenny it was easy to become part of the state and hard to get out. Jenny stayed with me about an hour, until I told her I would be okay and it was all right for her to leave.

After Jenny drove off, I stood in the front yard as tears begin to roll down my face, reliving the moment my children had suddenly been taken from me. After standing outside for a few minutes, I dreaded walking back into a quiet, gloomy house. I could feel their presence as I entered the door. I walked straight to my room where they had left their homework on the floor, their books open, backpacks and sweaters lying next to them. I sat on the edge of my bed wondering why. The tears began to flow uncontrollably. I could not take my clothes off. I just stared at what was left of the children. I picked their sweaters up off the floor and used them as a pillow, and continued to cry until I fell asleep.

On October 27, I had to call in sick to my job. I was mentally sick. I met our attorney downtown at the family court about noon.

In between cases, my attorney and I went before the judge. The attorney tried to explain to the judge about our case, but the judge said, "I have more important cases to worry about than yours. I will see you in two weeks on your appointed court date."

My attorney was almost put in jail for contempt because of the comment he made about the unfairness of the justice system.

I experienced the longest two weeks of my life. My oldest daughter routinely called every night, but for the strangest reason, she did not ask about the other kids during those two weeks. Before the kids left, she would call every night, asking to speak with her brother and asking about her sister. I wanted to tell her about her siblings being taken away, but I didn't want to interrupt her studies with family burdens. As we talked on the phone, I was on the other end crying silently, with tears rolling down my face.

As the days slowly went by, I did not stop my daily routine. The only thing different now was that my family was torn apart. I cried at night and smiled at work during the day and pretended my life was good. I did not tell my other coworkers because the situation was embarrassing. I worked for the state, and now I was a victim of the state. When my phone rang, I would go outside to the car and talk. Most of the time, it was our attorney. A coworker did get suspicious because I would leave the office to take my phone calls, whereas before, I would talk in my office. I would tell them that everything was fine, that I was just taking care of my personal call outside. I shared my story with only three people in my office. They had resources and information and helped in my situation.

On November 10, the evening before we were to go to court to find out if I was going to get my children back, I was driving home when an inspirational song came on the radio. The song came on right when I needed to hear it. While I was listening, I turned the radio up as loud as I could bear and started to sing along. At that point I was persuaded to *Trust God* for the return of my children.

Later that night my oldest daughter called as usual. This time when she called, I had an awkward feeling. I was afraid she would ask about the kids, but again she didn't ask. She sounded excited about school and life. I did not want to upset the one person in our family who was happy. After hanging up the phone, I called Jenny because Mary Louise had not answered when I'd tried her. I told her I hadn't told my oldest daughter about her siblings being taken away. Jenny said, "You need to let her know sooner or later!"

I decided to call my oldest daughter back that same night, and finally told her what had happened to the kids. She began to weep and blame herself for the situation. I told her not to blame herself and not to worry. After our conversation, I began to weep uncontrollably. In the back of my mind I could hear, Trust God. I went to bed.

On November 11, the judge granted the children's return home the next day by five o'clock. The judge did not understand why they had been taken in the first place. As we left the courtroom, our attorney rushed out ahead of us and went to the next room, weeping. He said that God answers prayers. The state would remain in our lives until further notice.

At five o'clock November 12, the children walked through the door, looking happy yet sad, too. God had a purpose and a plan for our lives. A few weeks before they had been removed from our home, I needed to get them new tennis shoes and new clothes, but I was waiting until the next payday. What the Devil meant for my evil, God made for my good. They returned home with enough clothes and tennis shoes to last them for a while. The Scripture says, "All things work together for the good of them who love the Lord." I love the Lord!

Chapter 3

The Truth Revealed

Maintaining my trust in God had become a habit I needed. I would get weak along the way, but God stayed right here. I know He is the same God yesterday, today, and forever more. However, I was very difficult to live a different life when things weren't normal.

You must be careful what you say because you can speak a thing into life, whether good or bad. We must also be careful how we treat our loved ones because we take them for granted, and when they are taken—and not by choice—we can reflect on the negative things we have said. We allow the Devil to plant negative seeds, and we allow those seeds to grow with doubt, unbelief, and negative talk. When you begin to think negative, begin to speak positive. Start praying and singing songs of victory.

The kids and I were settling down for the evening and a thought came to my mind to ask them what had happened on August 26, 2009. My son quickly responded, "Daddy did nothing to anyone." I asked him, how was that so? He said that his daddy was in his room the entire time. Then my daughter interrupted my son and said her daddy had done nothing. You could see the seriousness in their faces as they told minute by minute what had happened that day. It was as

The kids and I were settling down for the evening and a thought came to my mind to ask them what had happened on August 26, 2009. My son quickly responded, "Daddy did nothing to anyone." I asked him, how was that so? He said that his daddy was in his room the entire time. Then my daughter interrupted my son and said her daddy had done nothing. You could see the seriousness in their faces as they told minute by minute what had happened that day. It was as if they had been waiting for me to ask. I became very weak. That is when the other side of the story came to me.

Chapter 4

The Caseworker from Heaven

In spite of disastrous months, God always has a way of ending things right. By the end of the year, during the holidays, God provided us with a caseworker who thought all of this madness was ridiculous. I told him that my mother had sent him from heaven. He was very compassionate, and he believed in prayer. When we talked on the phone, he would always end our conversation with "Just keep praying."

At one of our meetings the caseworker asked me if I had spoken with my husband or the kids had spoken to their dad. I immediately responded no. He said he didn't understand why my husband had been asked to leave in the first place. He allowed the family to slowly come back together.

I know for a fact that a family that prays together stays together. Prayer is what we did daily at home. Before we did our daily travel, we always prayed. Sometimes we allowed the children to pray. As I reflected on that year, I noticed that I prayed more than I had the previous year. I began to trust and depend on God to work things out for me. My feelings were mixed. Sometimes I was confused. I wanted to escape to a depressed state of mind. My mind was kept together by the thought of my family's well-being.

2010

Chapter 5

The Return Home

As always, I hosted a New Year's Day dinner on January 1. After my mother passed in 1989, I kept the traditional dinner going. The menu consisted of chitterlings and hog maws, mustard greens with salt jowl, black-eyed peas, sweet potatoes, cornbread, and, new on the menu, gumbo. Later that day we ended with fried chicken.

Usually we had friends and family come over for dinner, played cards, and watched football all day. With this situation going on, things were somewhat different. We invited guests as always and had our party like always. We enjoyed ourselves and bore the hurt. We just did not want anyone to know about our family situation. We always had a smile.

My husband had been gone two months, and although the kids and I were surviving mentally with him not in the house, we missed him every day. I started to feel like a single parent. I was afraid that my feelings for him would go away, but I kept the focus on the fact that he was my husband, the father of my children, and that the truth had to be told.

On January 10, an earthquake destroyed the country of Haiti. The military was deployed from the United States to Haiti in a rescue mission to assist in rebuilding the country.

My husband got the opportunity to go to Haiti. It was good for him to get away from the situation and do what he has always done best: help people.

The state continued to be part of our lives. We had to visit with a therapist on a weekly basis and were instructed to take parenting classes. Since my husband was gone, I was going to take the classes alone. I was just waiting for the date for them to begin.

In February I had to go to court, where the judge asked how long we had been parents. "Eighteen years," I replied. He chuckled and said we did not need parenting classes. I started thinking to myself, *this judge is not so bad after all.*

The caseworker said, "I don't see how this case went this far, after I read the case summary of the situation, it does not make sense." He would tell me, "Just keep praying God is going to work it out." He told me he would do his best to reunite our family. Another court date was set for March.

I prayed before going to court, that the judge would dismiss the case and allow for my husband to return home from his duty in Haiti.

In March the judge granted that our case would be dismissed on April 14, my birthday. He said I did not need to come back to court.

God had answered my prayer. In May when everything was officially over with CPS, my husband returned home and was able to reunite with his us once again.

Chapter 6

Allegation One Indictment

The state was no longer a part of our lives on the civil side of the court system, but we still had to deal with the criminal side. We prayed and hoped that it would go away too. Our attorney waited to hear from law enforcement so that they could question my husband about the allegations. He never received a call.

In August, the criminal justice system became a part of our lives. Instead of a phone call from law enforcement, my husband got a warrant for his arrest. Once I found out that the charge was an aggravated felony charge, I knew I needed to act quickly because he could be arrested at his job or at home. He did not need the embarrassment at his job, and my children didn't need to go through anything else with law enforcement. They had already been through enough.

I had to think fast. I needed to call someone who was familiar with the process of getting a bond. I called an associate of mine. My associate told me I was going to need money now. I began to think about how we were going to get money.

I thought about getting a payday loan. I mentioned it to my husband. He put his head down because he had always been against payday loans. Now it was his only option. He had always believed in saving money and in having rainy-day money. His savings were tied up and there would be a penalty for withdrawal now. To get money immediately, he had to do a title loan against his truck for his bond.

I really had to think about this situation because now it was serious. It wasn't that it hadn't been serious before, but we were talking about going to jail and a thirty-thousand-dollar bond. If convicted, my husband would go to prison for twenty-five years to life.

I felt my whole life crumbling. I became weak and felt like crying, but I had to keep a straight face so that my true emotions wouldn't show while I was sitting in my office. Being in the middle of the criminal justice system was a beast. I followed my associate's advice and began the criminal justice journey.

I had to learn about how the bonding process worked. I had never dealt with a bond at this level. I did my research on the bonding process:

> Bail is a process through which an arrested criminal suspect pays a set amount of money to obtain release from police custody, usually after booking. As a condition of release, the suspect promises to appear in court for all scheduled criminal proceedings — including arraignment, preliminary hearing, and pre-trial Motions, and the trial itself. If the suspect fails to appear in court as scheduled, he or she will be subject to immediate arrest, and any bail amount paid will be forfeited.

After understanding how the bonding system works, I understood what had to take place after each court date. My husband had to check in with the bonding company weekly, and if he wanted to travel, he had to get a travel permit.

I thought to myself, *one day you are free to make choices in life and the next you are chained to the justice system, with limited choices.*

Well, since we were in this together, I had to keep

believing we would come out of it together in victory. But my biggest question was *when?*

Chapter 7

What Did I Do Wrong?

When I married my husband twenty-one years ago, he had no criminal record, and now there was an aggravated felony charge pending against him.

We drove home from court in pure silence. There was no radio—just the sound of the outside world. It was eating at my mind that I needed to ask him again what had happened on August 26, 2009, but the thought of the hurtfulness would not allow me to open my mouth. I kept driving in silence.

We arrived home and went straight to the bedroom, not for an evening of pleasure but to get the truth out. As I looked into his eyes, I said softly, "Please tell me the truth."

With tears in his eyes, he replied, "I did nothing to hurt anyone. I didn't know what happened until you told me. I just want to retire from the military and take care of my family."

I sat down beside him and began to weep.

Later that night after everyone was in bed, I needed some comforting words, so I called Mary Louise. "What did we do wrong?" I asked.

"You have done nothing wrong," she said. "You have been faithful to God, and He won't forget about your faithfulness."

I accepted those words of comfort and went to sleep peacefully.

Chapter 8

A Continual Prayer

On August 16, we went to court for the first time. We both were very nervous, not knowing what to expect. The judge told my husband what he was accused of and asked him how he intended to plead. "Not guilty, Your Honor," my husband said. The judge gave him a reset because he did not have an attorney and did not qualify for a court-appointed attorney. He was given almost thirty days to hire an attorney. The judge was somewhat aggressive toward my husband, as though my husband had been proven guilty. What had happened to "innocent until proven guilty"? My husband and I were starting to feel like this was going to be the end of our lives in the justice system—at least it appeared that way.

I had some knowledge and understanding of what was going on, but remember, I work in the criminal justice system, so to broaden my prior knowledge and understanding, I began to research this type of aggravated case so that I would understand what might have happened. I remembered that in Proverbs 4:5, it says, "Get wisdom, get understanding: forget it not" (KJV).

I surrounded myself with people who were knowledgeable about this type of case. I knew it was going to be a long journey.

I was careful about whom I discussed my family situation with because it was very embarrassing and was not something to be discussed. Mary Louise would always say,

"Don't tell everybody your business." Therefore, I talked with only a few people. This was a situation in which prayer, faith, trust, facts, and speaking the truth were the only way out!

As the days went by, I would experience weakness in my mind. I would think the worst of the worst. I would replay August 26, 2009, in my mind every day, picturing him guilty, but while the events of the day seem to point back to his innocence. I recalled telling him on that day, "Go straight to your room and lock the door in your own house." He had even had second thoughts about coming home that day. He said, "I don't like this but I will go home."

I would pray until the thoughts went away. I would think about my mother-in-law and how she loved my family. Then I would think about how my children were taken from me and were gone for only two weeks. I thanked God for the long two weeks without them. Before they left, I would say, "I need a vacation from you all." Yep, I got a vacation all right, a forced vacation. And sometimes I would say to my husband, "Why don't you just leave sometime." Yep: be careful what you ask for. He left, all right! He was gone away not by choice but because he was forced to leave for about five months.

Chapter 9

My New Life

At nine o'clock in the morning, September 10, 2010, we sat, waiting for them to call the docket. I looked around the courtroom, wondering if I would see someone I knew. *Nope, not this time.* My husband did not have an attorney, and the judge said she would put him in jail if he did not get one. She asked that we bring a financial statement to court to prove we were indigent and needed a court-appointed attorney. There went another reset within two weeks of that day. We had to leave the courtroom and go to the bonding company so that he could check in and make a payment on his bond.

At nine o'clock in the morning on September 17, we sat waiting for them to call the docket. I did the same thing I had done on September 10, scoping out the courtroom for someone I knew. *Nope, not this time.* My husband gave the judge the requested financial statement and she said we made too much money to qualify for a court-appointed attorney. He tried to explain that we could not afford an attorney, but she replied, "If you don't bring an attorney on your next court date, we will arrange one for you while you sit in jail." Another court date was set. I walked out of the courtroom feeling defeated with an onset of depression.

As I sat waiting for him while he checked in at the bonding company, I called Mary Louise to give her the update. She asked if it was over yet, and I told her we had gotten another court date. She said, "Well, we will keep praying."

I prayed and thought to myself, *I want this over now. I don't know how long I can take this.* Her words would always make me regroup and start thinking of hope.

We met with our first attorney, not knowing that he would not be our last. We went through the protocol of the legal system, hired him, and gave him a retainer fee. We couldn't afford an attorney at this time, but God provided us with the resources to pay for it by way of my husband's 401(k). This was not his way of spending his hard-earned money, but he wanted to do what he needed to do hire an attorney. That was one indication of his innocence.

As the attorney asked my husband questions about the allegation, he listened, then stopped him from talking, and said, "You did not commit this crime." I wanted to know how he knew that. He explained how my husband was innocent. I sat contemplating the attorney and how he had concluded that my husband was innocent. He said he would get the case dismissed but wanted his money.

We started to feel a little hope and went home happy. In the back of my mind, we were not free. We still had another court date set. I was thinking; *well, maybe next time it will get dismissed.* I became spiritually weak, but I had to remember to trust God. I would quote Matthew 6:33, "But seek ye first the kingdom of God, and his righteousness; and all these things shall be added unto you" (KJV). I knew that would do it! Just as He had answered my prayer the first time, He would do it again.

We went through the same routine at nine o'clock, October 25. They called the docket. I still felt like I was going to see someone I knew, but now I was starting to feel like we were the only ones who had problems. That day was not so bad: everyone before us had their changes dismissed. I thought, *this is the day*. I started to pray silently, "Dear God, I believe your word. I trust you, so dismiss, dismiss, dismiss." I said *dismiss* three times: one for the Father, one for the Son, and one for the Holy Ghost. I thought this was the day our case would be dismissed.

Our attorney showed up, and now it was his and my husband's turn to approach the bench. My heart started to beat faster and faster. The district attorney read off the charges, and I heard the judge ask, "How do you plead?"

My husband replied, "I am innocent, Your Honor." But the attorney asked for a reset to give him time to prepare for trial. I sat back on the bench, hurt. In my mind, I said, "God, what are you doing? Another reset?" I felt like God had failed me.

I became angry with the attorney and the judge. I wanted to stand up and say, "Your Honor, you know this man didn't do anything." I looked at the judge and then over at the attorney and thought, *why is she being so mean to him, and why did they do a reset?* Another thought came to mind: *The attorney didn't ask for a dismissal like everyone else.* I watched the attorney walk over to the court clerk and pick up a yellow-and-green paper. He walked toward us and pointed toward the door. We got up and walked out behind him into a small room. He told us we owed him a balance and handed my husband the piece of paper with a new court date in November.

On November 29, it was the same routine. We were back at the courthouse, there was the docket call, and I looked around for anyone I knew and thought, *nope — nobody I know.* My husband still owed the attorney a small balance, so we got another reset. My husband was waiting for the money from his 401(k) to arrive so he could pay the attorney.

It was a very slow process. I spoke with Greta, who said, "Be prepared. This is going to be a long process, and it's going to get worse." Greta was a dear friend of mine from work that was very resourceful to me.

"The attorney said he could get it dismissed," I responded.

"This type of case is hard to beat," she said. I felt crushed inside when I heard that. I continued to hold on to the truth. Reminiscing, I could hear the little voice saying, "He didn't do anything!" That was my hope at time, and it made me smile.

On December 27, we went through the same routine as the previous month. This time the attorney was paid in full. I began to repeat in my mind while sitting in the courtroom, *Dismiss, dismiss, dismiss.* The attorney walked in, went to the court clerk's desk, walked back to us, and had us follow him out the door into the little room. He said, "Well, this is going to trial."

I wanted to just scream. "Why?" I asked.

"The state is just following orders," he said. *Following orders,* I thought. I didn't ask any more questions. We told him good-bye and that we'd see him next month.

While we were going to the bonding company to report, we started talking about how this could be the end of our lives. What if this happened? What if that happened?

What I needed was some encouraging words from Mary Louise. While waiting for my husband to get back into the car, I called her. I kept a calm voice as I wiped away the tears of hurt and pain in my heart. All she said was "God is going to bring you all out of this." I thought, *she always says that.* But I needed to start keeping the faith and believing that God was going to bring us out. It was not that I didn't believe, but I was caught up in my emotions and feeling sorry for myself. Sometimes I thought, *This could be my fault. If I had done this or if I had done that, we would not be here.* But eventually, I began to think, *Maybe God has a plan.*

As I reflected at the end of the year, I realized it was

interesting: it was to my advantage to be working as an officer. I had many resources to assist me through the devastating events of the year. I prayed, "Please, God, take the problem away. It hurts my heart." I reminisced about the day we went to court. I had been very scared because it was my first experience dealing with the justice system at that level. I continued to claim that the case would be dismissed, based on facts and truth.

2011

Chapter 10

Allegation Two Revealed and Case Dismissed

On January 1, I hosted at my home. It was our traditional New Year's Party, and we celebrated Mary Louise's birthday. We had a wonderful time.

As the next court date neared, we continued to live every day as if it was going to be our last. I would replay August 26, 2009, in the back of my mind, trying to put things in order. Each time this happened, Mary Louise would call with encouraging words, trying to help me stay focused for the family. She would call my husband and give encouraging words to him as well. She would tell us not to tell everybody our business because this was our personal matter.

On January 25, we went to court doing the same routine. This time the judge asked that we return the next day, January 26. We returned the next day, and the judge set the pretrial for February 24 and the trial for March 11. When I heard the words *pretrial* and *trial,* I felt that all hope was gone. I said to God, "Lord, I prayed for dismissal, and You're allowing this to go to trial." I became very angry. I had to just hold all of it inside. I wanted to tell the judge that my husband was innocent. I wanted to tell her the other side of the story.

An outburst like that would have landed me in jail. I just held it all in.

The district attorney offered ten years' prison time, but my husband rejected it without a counteroffer. Our attorney said, "No, we are not taking anything but a trial."

My husband said, "If I take a plea bargain, it is saying that I am guilty." He looked at the attorney and me, saying, "I did nothing to anyone."

As the days slowly went by, it became a more difficult time. I began to cry secretly. I needed to get enough strength to pray.

"Just hold on. God is going to see you through this," Mary Louise kept saying.

In the early part of February, I went into a new ministry. I became an Internet radio disc jockey playing gospel music on Sunday mornings. This opportunity couldn't have come at a better time. It was what I needed to keep me going. Although we had the pretrial and trial dates set, I was thinking positive and thinking dismissal.

I had the chance to talk to an old friend of mine. I looked up his phone number and called him. He was so encouraging. He was trying to strategize how to stop the case from going to court. He said he would talk to some people and maybe they could help us. We talked every day.

On February 24, my husband went to court for the pretrial, this time without me. I went to work hoping he would call to say the case was dismissed. I got a call from him while I was at the office. I could hear in his voice that he was very frightened. He said there was a new district attorney and that the attorney wanted him to sign papers for probation.

"Please come down here. I don't know what the attorney is doing. I am not signing for something I did not do," he told me.

I told my office manager that I needed to leave on an emergency. I rushed out of my office discreetly and drove

downtown in emergency mode. I finally arrived at the courtroom and found my husband almost pale. I approached the attorney and asked him what was going on. The attorney explained what he needed to do if he got convicted.

"This is not a plea bargain?" I asked.

"No," he replied.

I told the attorney to give me a few minutes. We did not trust the criminal justice system. I called one of my sources. My source assured me that it was okay to sign, and my husband signed the documentation. This would allow him the chance to take probation if the case went to trial and he was found guilty. It was just part of the procedure in the pretrial.

Between February 24 and March 7, I received a call from Anthony, an old friend. We carried on a conversation for about two weeks. While communication with him evolved, an interesting piece of evidence was revealed that would hurt the credibility of the prosecution. It was so disturbing that I am ashamed to discuss it. This was a mental setback for my family. We had to regroup and pray. We had to immediately turn the evidence over to our attorney so that we would not be held accountable for keeping it in our possession.

On March 7, I received a phone call from Anthony, not knowing it would be my last call from him. All of a sudden he ceased calling. He just stopped communicating with me. I don't know what happened.

On March 11, we went downtown for the trial. I kept praying for a dismissal. I kept saying it in my mind.

As we were going up to the courtroom on the elevator, the attorney got on and said that a new allegation had surfaced. "I know what that is about," my oldest daughter said. My youngest daughter had told me early in the year to expect a new allegation. This was another setback for the family.

I continued to believe that we were going to get a dismissal that day. My husband was in the courtroom with his attorney while my daughter and I waited in the small room. I just wanted to lie flat on the floor while I continued to say "Dismissal" in my mind. A few minutes later, my husband and the attorney walked through the door. Both said, "Dismissal!"

My daughter and I started to weep.

"But it is subject to re-filing," the attorney said.

"What does that mean?" I asked.

He said, "That they dismissed it because the district attorney was not prepared, being that she just got the case last month."

"So does this mean it is over?" I asked.

"It is possible that they can re-file," he said.

"Okay, so when might they re-file?" I asked.

"Maybe thirty days or more" was his answer.

We came home that day feeling really good. We told the kids about the dismissal. They were very excited. We all went and sat outside on the deck in the backyard. We had not been out in the back in a while because we had not had the freedom or spirit to do so. We just sat and looked into the blue skies and were thankful to God for allowing this to be over.

As the days slowly went by, we were trying to adjust back to normal living. In the back of my mind I was not totally satisfied. I had the weird feeling that something was not right, but I could not recognize what. I was stuck on the word *re-file*. But I just kept being thankful.

Chapter 11

Arrested

At approximately 6:30 a.m. April 7, I walked past the window in the foyer of my home and noticed five police officers standing outside my door. I opened the door and asked, "May I help you?" They nicely moved me out of the way and said they were looking for my husband. With guns pointed at me, they walked into the house. I told them he was just getting out of the shower and getting dressed for work. They went to the bathroom, pointing their guns, and told him they were there for him and to get dressed because he was going to jail.

I told the police officers that they did not have to point their guns at me and that I was an officer and had no reason to break the law. I was totally insulted! One of the officers actually apologized to me. He said he was just doing his job. I tried to keep the kids out of the way as they handcuffed their dad. My youngest daughter came downstairs anyway and told the officer, "You don't have to do all that with my daddy because of lies told about him."

The officer apologized to her and said, "I am just doing my job." They needed to get my driver's license information and told me what I needed to do to get him out of jail. I thought to myself, *I don't have any money.*

After they left with my husband, the kids and I sat down for a minute to digest what just happened to our family. I felt like it was a nightmare and I was going to wake up when it was over, but it was real.

I needed to work fast to try to get him out of jail that same day. We had no money. I could not ask anyone because it was embarrassing. I could not think. But I had to get it together because I needed to call his job to let them know what was happening. I called my job and told them I was sick and could not come to work. I was mentally sick. I felt like I was not going to survive all of this. I could not give up because I had to get him out of jail and I have children. Then the thought came to my mind: *This is too much for someone who always tried to do the right thing.* I was caught up in thoughts of disbelief.

I finally calmed down enough to call my source to help me through the process of getting him out of jail. I was thinking about the money again and where I was going to get what I needed to get him out. I thought to myself, *Tomorrow is his payday, but that means he will have to stay overnight.* Then I became angry. He would have to sit in jail because of not only one lie but now two lies. Because of all the indications that led me to believe the allegations were not true, I could not let him sit in jail. That was what motivated me to get my thoughts together and call the right bonding company that would work with the money he was going to get from his paycheck. I found one that would work with me.

The evening finally came and the kids were quiet. We did not turn on the TV. We did not eat at the dinner table. This was going to be a long night.

In April 6, we made the effort to make it a normal day in spite of the missing link in our family. The kids went to school, and I went and paid the bonding company with just enough because his military check came just in time. I finally went on to work. Later that morning while I was sitting in my office, my husband called from the jail. I didn't want my coworkers to know what was happening with my family. I

I left the office to speak with him in my car. I became sad after hearing his voice. The first thing I asked him was if he was okay. He replied that he was okay but wanted to get out. I told him I had already started the process. I could hear sadness in his voice. After hanging up the phone I began to weep silently and asked God to help us get through the situation.

I left my office again to go sit in the car to try to call our attorney. I finally got in touch with him, and he was not surprised to hear that the district attorney had re-filed the case. I asked him what we should do next. He replied, "I will need another four thousand dollars to get started." I told him I did not have any money. "You all might qualify for a court-appointed attorney," he said. All I could think about was my husband taking a plea bargain and going to prison for something he did not do if we got a court-appointed attorney. We ended the conversation with the attorney saying, "If you get four thousand dollars, call me. Good luck to you."

After hanging up the phone, I could not think beyond the conversation. I felt defeated and did not want to pray or ask God for anything. I finally called Mary Louise and told her what had happened. She became very angry. "This is ridiculous, and it needs to stop," she said. "Just keep praying and believing in God."

I asked her, "What did we do wrong for this to happen to us?"

"God is going to work this out," she replied. "Just keep holding on."

As the evening approached, I called downtown at the jail to see if my husband was ready to be released. It was a long process. Finally, I called again later that evening, and he was ready.

While parked outside the booking and releasing side of the jail, I sat in my car in disbelief. I could not believe I was waiting for my husband to be released from jail. I began to think, *What am I doing here?* I wondered how he might be feeling, having his life interrupted by this situation.

While waiting for my husband, I called Mary Louise so she could give me encouraging words. She was always good at believing that God would bring you out. She said, "God won't put any more on you than you can bear."

I told her that this was a very hard test and I might not pass it.

"Oh yeah, you are going to pass the test," she said. "You just hang in there."

While I was sitting there in an incomprehensible situation, my nerves were jolted when I got a call from an unknown number. Thoughts of whom it might be passed through my mind like wildfire, and I had an intense urge to answer. So I did. "Hello?"

"Hey, where are you?" said my husband's familiar voice on the other end. As I replied to him, a bittersweet feeling made my heart beat at an uncontrollably high rate, but the fact that I was speaking to him made me focus all my concern on him. While finishing the conversation, he spotted me and walked toward the car. I noticed he had borrowed someone's cell phone to call me. Even though I did not want to let him go, I hung up after realizing he was coming near the car. He got in, and as I glanced at him and patted his knee, I asked, "Are you okay?"

"Yes," he replied. "I am just glad to be out of there, and I don't want to go back."

We had to stop by the bonding company for him to check in. While waiting on him at the bonding company I began to blame myself for his being in this situation. *If I could have … I should have, but I didn't. Maybe we should move out of town like we once discussed,* I thought. *If I had listened to him sometimes and not been so worried about my reputation, we would not be in this type of situation.* These were the things that came to mind as I blamed myself. ___

As I waited, I called Mary Louise again and began to tell her how I was feeling. She immediately begins to pray. After her prayer, I felt a weight being lifted off of me. My husband returned to the car, and we finally begin to head toward home.

As we were riding, I didn't know what to say to him. I thought about the attorney. I told him that the attorney wanted more money because two more cases had been added. My husband said he didn't have any money. I told him I did not want us to get a court-appointed attorney. I told him I would call a friend to see if he knew an attorney who would allow us to do a payment plan. We had to think fast because the next court date was coming soon.

Chapter 12

Questionable Prayers and Discord in the Courtroom

It was April 15, and we went to court, this time without an attorney. The atmosphere in the courtroom was positive. It was another morning when everyone was getting their cases dismissed. I thought to myself, *This is going to be the day. Dismiss, dismiss, dismiss.* It was time for my husband to go before the judge. I sat in almost a cold sweat, repeating, "Dismiss" to myself several times.

I notice that the district attorney had changed. I thought, *Oh yes, this is it. I can feel it.* But at the same time, doubt was doing an excellent job on me. My husband told the judge that our attorney wanted to charge him again for the case but under a different case number. The judge became very upset and told him he needed to file a complaint against the attorney. She told my husband to bring our tax statements for the previous three years to see if we qualified for assistance with his legal expenses. The court date was reset again. I sat in disbelief. I just wanted to scream really loud, I kept it in because an outburst would have sent me to jail.

I started to wonder if my prayers worked. I knew how strongly I believed in God and that He could do anything but fail. But this was beginning to get a little ridiculous. We walked out of the courtroom feeling overwhelmed.

Later in April I thought things had to get better. Well, they didn't. The kids and I were home from our daily routine of work and school when there was a knock at the door. I opened the door and it was the repo people coming to pick up my car. I told the person I had been paying monthly, although I was behind. I had communicated with the finance company, and they had told me to continue making the car payment until I could send an extra one.

I gave them the key, went to the garage, and cleaned out the car with the help of the children. My son wanted to know why they were taking the car. I explained to him why and he responded, "It's okay, Mama; we will get another one." I wanted to cry, but I had to keep a straight face for them. I did not want them to see me upset. I had to keep an upbeat attitude in spite of my car getting repossessed. This would mean we were down to one vehicle making five different stops, with bad tires and no air conditioner. It was already hot. I felt defeated.

As the end of April approached, we gathered our tax information for the previous three years. I thought, *The judge will not give him a court-appointed attorney with the money we have made in the last three years* — money we could not save because of the legal bills we had inherited, not by choice.

Chapter 13

Financial Statement Review

On May 10, we were back in court. My thought was *Dismiss, dismiss, dismiss.* The judge called up my husband to review our financial statements. I sat, looking and waiting for her to respond to what she was reading. She asked my husband a few questions about our income. She then spoke sarcastically, saying, "I see your wife is an officer."

He replied, "Yes, Your Honor."

After she finished reviewing everything, she said to my husband, "You can afford an attorney. Have one here at the next court date or I will put you in jail so that you can get a court-appointed attorney." I just closed my eyes, imagining my husband sitting in jail. I thought, *If he sits in jail, he'll lose his job. Then I'll have to get another job, but if he takes a plea bargain, we would not have to spend any more money.* Then I thought about the consequences of taking a plea bargain: he would be labeled as a criminal. Well, that won't work. *How about if I just pray and trust God?*

As we left the courtroom, I wanted to fall on the floor. Again, I thought of making a scene. Maybe the judge would feel sorry for us and just dismiss the case. In all reality we know that is not how it works, so I just kept walking out the door.

I called Mary Louise for encouragement. She told me

to keep praying and trusting God — like I didn't already know to do that. She went on to say that the judge needed to go ahead and dismiss the case because the allegations were not true. Now, that is what I needed to hear because it let me know there was still hope and that I had to believe God was going to work things out.

Chapter 14

The New Attorney

A few days went by and we still did not have a clue who was going to be our new attorney. On a whim, I called my old friend Luther. I knew he was a praying person, and I was led to tell him what was going on in my family. He was very hurt to hear about the situation. I told him we needed an attorney. He began to tell me about a former juvenile judge who was currently practicing criminal law, and gave me her contact information.

I called the former judge. I began to tell her what happened and she interrupted me, saying, "That did not happen."

"How do you know?"

"Years of experience have allowed me to recognize this type of allegation and determine the difference," she said. She asked that we come to her office to further discuss the case.

Two days later my husband, my oldest daughter, and I met with the former judge at her office. We gave her the evidence we had received from the previous attorney, and then she listened to our side of the story. After we all told everything we knew, she said, "It's impossible that he did this. The stories are inconsistent." She said she would do her best to get the case dismissed but that it would probably go to trial.

When I heard the word *trial*, all I could think of was prison. I could not think beyond that. I was very much aware that this type of case was very hard to win. Although she told us positive things, I just could not see us winning. My stomach began to twist in a knot while I tried to keep a smile on my face and stay positive.

She gave us her contract with a payment plan, and we signed it and hired our second attorney.

In June I was assigned to go to training for my job. I would miss the next court date. I didn't want to miss the court date, but I was glad to get away. I needed to get away. I thought, *This would be the perfect time for a miracle to happen.* My hope was shifting to *Dismiss* again.

Chapter 15

The Money Came Too Late

We needed to make the first payment to the attorney at the next court date, which was a few days away. My husband needed to get some money. I suggested that he get another title loan. This was a painful thing for him to do. "I just don't want to get another title loan," he said.

I said to him, "Well, what do you want to do: get a loan or sit in jail?" He looked at me with defeat in his eyes. I said, "If you didn't do anything, you have to fight."

"I have not hurt anybody, and it is not fair that I have to get money for something like this."

"Just do what you've got to do." We were starting to feel the financial burden this situation was putting us in.

He procrastinated about applying for the loan, and the money would not be available until after noon on June 21. He was due to have the attorney's first payment at the court setting.

On June 21, my husband was back in court and I was in training out of town. I was there thinking, Dismiss, dismiss, dismiss. My focus was not on the training. I was waiting for the phone call from him. With the intensity of my anxiety, my heart began to beat slowly and my left leg seemed to capture a huge piece of the emotion, shaking uncontrollably.

Finally, my phone vibrated. I knew it was him calling. I quietly excused myself from the training and stepped outside. As I spoke with him, I walked down the walkway just in case I needed to scream when he said that it had been dismissed. As he started to talk, I could hear the disappointment in his voice. "The attorney is getting off the case," he said.

"Why? What happened?" I asked in disbelief.

He took a breath and then replied, "I did not have the money, and she felt like we would not be able to pay her. She strongly suggests that I get a court-appointed attorney."

As I listened on the other end of the line, my true emotions had me confused and wanting to scream or just sit on the ground and cry. I wanted to lash out at him for not getting the loan on time. In the heat of the moment I did not know how to feel or how to respond. Although I was upset with my husband, I knew that if I wanted a positive outcome, I had to remain positive and calm. As I held the phone to my ear, I began to think that if I had been there, none of this would have happened, but I failed to realize that, like always, God had a purpose and a plan.

As I listened on the other end of the line, my true emotions had me confused and wanting to scream or just sit on the ground and cry. I wanted to lash out at him for not getting the loan on time. In the heat of the moment I did not know how to feel or how to respond. Although I was upset with my husband, I knew that if I wanted a positive outcome, I had to remain positive and calm. As I held the phone to my ear, I began to think that if I had been there, none of this would have happened, but I failed to realize that, like always, God had a purpose and a plan.

Isaiah 5:8 (NIV) came to mind: "For my thoughts are not your thoughts, neither are your ways my ways." Therefore, how was I supposed to know God's plan and what He had ahead for me?

My husband confirmed: "The attorney was very popular in the courtroom among her peers." He also said that the attorney had asked the judge for a reset because she was new to the case. The attorney knew she was not going to represent him, but she carried on like she was, he said. The court date was reset.

My husband went on to get a second title loan, and we were again on the market to hire an attorney. We went day after day, trying to think of someone to hire. We had a few friends and relatives who were attorneys, but it would have been a conflict of interest to use them because of their personal relationship with my family.

Chapter 16

A Chance We Will Take

A few days before the next court date, I suggested to my husband that he talk with his union attorney. "I don't know if she does criminal law," he said, so I asked him to find out.

Later that day she called back. He told her what was going on. She told him she did not do criminal law. My husband was convinced that she could handle his case, and she wanted to meet with us.

A few days later the attorney came to the house and we sat at the breakfast table to talk. I left the area, and she talked to my husband first. Their conversation was not very long because he did not have much to say about what was going on. He told her what he was accused of and continued to say that he hadn't done anything to anyone. She then talked to the kids. She spoke with my son first. Their conversation was short. He told what he needed to tell, the truth. Then she spoke to my youngest daughter. Their conversation was somewhat long because she told the attorney something she needed to reveal about the situation. She knew to tell the truth.

From the beginning of my children's lives we instilled the importance of always being honest. They sometimes got punished for being untruthful. My mother would tell me that if I told a story, I would die and go to the Devil (hell). My father told me one day while I was growing up, "Baby, whatever you do, tell the truth. Always tell the truth."

It was my turn to talk with the attorney. As I began to talk with her, I became angry because we were trapped in this situation. I began to share with her some of the things I had experienced and the reason we were going through this. I then calmed down and began to cry because I was so hurt. My heart was heavy because I had only tried to do the right things in life, and now I was in this situation.

After talking with me, she called for my husband to return to the table. She told us she had never been on this type of case and did not feel comfortable taking it. My husband told her that he thought she should take it. I told her the same thing. I just felt within me that she needed to challenge herself. I even thought she could win the case for us if she did what we asked her to do.

The attorney met with us again to tell us how much she would charge to represent us. Of course, we did not have the money. We told her we wanted to hire her. She said she would work with us on the payment.

We believed that God would make a way for us to pay her. We were expecting some money from a hurricane settlement. We did not have an exact date, but we knew it was coming. I was confident that she would get paid.

On July 12, we were back in court. Going to court was routine. This was the first time the new attorney went to court with us. She was very nervous, and the judge called them to the bench. I could not hear a lot, but from what I gathered, they were talking about setting the pretrial date and a trial date. I was somewhat relaxed because I felt good about this attorney. I adjusted to the fact that a dismissal does not come easily. The state was instructed to proceed with the case. When I heard that, my heart hurt. The next court date was set.

Chapter 17

No Food

We carried on with our lives as normally as possible. Knowing that we were walking hand in hand with the state kept our freedom trapped. Our finances sometimes would not allow us to buy groceries. Sometimes we had enough money to buy a bag of chicken, which would last about two days. Then we ate egg sandwiches for about three days. It was funny because the kids were content with what we had to eat at the time. Then I would get a call from a longtime friend asking if we needed anything. I was embarrassed to say that we did not have any food. Her motherly instinct would recognize that we were in need and she would drive up with a trunk full of groceries.

Another friend of mine called and casually asked, "What are you cooking today?"

Embarrassed, I slowly replied, "Nothing. We don't have any food."

"I am on my way." About thirty-five minutes later she came knocking at my front door with bags of groceries and said, "Don't be without food again. You'd better call me." God always has a ram in the bush.

Chapter 18

Always a Ram in the Bush

God placed another friend in our lives to financially assist my family on a weekly basis. After that we did not have to worry about food in our house.

The new attorney was really on her job; however, she would seek another attorney to assist her with our case.

We felt like if she just did what we asked her to do, she would be fine. Well, she didn't. She got an associate of hers to assist her. She brought him by the house, and we sat down at the breakfast table and talked with him. He said we needed an investigator and that maybe we could get the state to compensate us for the fees. He also said we would need a psychologist to come and testify during the trial. I was thinking to myself, maybe he won't be so bad after all. He sounded like he knew what he was talking about.

A few days later, the investigator came by and spoke to all five of us: my husband and me and the three kids. She spoke with us individually. She made us feel very comfortable and told us everything was going to be all right. She gave us an overview of our stories and said that the charges made in this case could not possibly be true. I just sat and looked at her. "How do you know?" I asked.

"I am very familiar with this type of case because I was a victim myself," she said.

The attorney came to the house again to let my husband know what to expect at the next court date.

Chapter 19

Plea Bargain Offer

On August 16, we went to court. It was the same routine, except now it was becoming serious. The co-attorney did not get off to a good start with the judge. They exchanged some heated words, and the judge asked him to visit with her at another date as soon as possible. The co-attorney agreed to visit with the judge. I became very nervous because I didn't know what was going on. This co-attorney was going to send my husband to prison. I watched the district attorney and our attorney exchange words, and then they were laughing and talking. It was making me angry on the inside, but then I thought to myself, *Maybe this is a good sign. Maybe we might get a dismissal.* Well, it was just another day in court. The attorneys walked toward us and said we had another reset with three different dates. After hearing that, I just wanted to pass out.

Our attorney checked her calendar to let us know when she would visit with us to prepare for the trial. The co-attorney appeared upset and did not stay long after leaving the courtroom.

My husband said to our attorney, "You can do this. I have faith that you will be fine if you just listen to what my wife and I tell you."

She replied, "This is a very serious case, and I am not comfortable doing this alone. Our next court date is like a pretrial and then there's the trial."

I asked our attorney how it was looking. She said the district attorney believed the allegations were true and was moving forward with the trial. Our attorney also said the district attorney wanted to give my husband twenty to ninety-nine years in prison if he was convicted, since my husband wanted to go to trial. I became angry. I was wondering how they could convict someone without hearing the other side of the story.

My husband was very calm. He said, "If I have to go to prison, I will go standing for the truth. I know I did nothing wrong." He continued to talk with tears his eyes: "My daddy always told my brothers and me to stand for the truth, and that is what I am going to do."

I said, "Well, if you didn't do anything, we must continue to fight until the end."

Over the next few days, life was not happy around our home. We believe in our faith and trusted God, but reality would kick in and make us sad and angry. We were living paycheck to paycheck. Paying to live in our house was becoming hard to do. We were unable to make our mortgage payments. I kept in contact with the mortgage company, keeping them posted on our situation.

We had been through three loan modifications just to buy time. We had made about three house payments that year. We were driving the hell out of our one vehicle. The tires were getting worse, and the summer was long and extremely hot.

A few days before the next court date, our attorney came by the house to visit with us and discuss a plea bargain. She wanted to let my husband know that a plea bargain was being offered. She didn't want to be held responsible if my husband decided to change his mind.

While we were discussing the plea bargain, our attorney called one of our attorney friends to help persuade my husband to take the plea bargain. He was placed on speakerphone so that we could all hear the conversation. He told us all the disadvantages of not taking the plea bargain. He said we would lose our house, and if we went to trial and didn't win, my husband would go to prison. Last, if there was a hung jury, the cost to get the transcript would be very expensive, and we would not be able to afford it.

My husband just sat and looked at me with a strong face. He turned and said to his attorney, "I did not do anything to anyone. Why would I take a plea bargain?"

He said to our attorney friend, "We will just have to deal with it because I am not taking a plea bargain!"

I told our attorney friend, "We can get another house if we lose this one. It is a chance we will have to take."

My husband signed the notification declining the plea bargain.

Chapter 20

I Can't Take It

September 13, finally came, and we were back in court to start preparing for the trial. Our attorney and her co-attorney were both present. The judge immediately asked the assisting attorney why he had not visited with her to discuss the case, and he gave an excuse. I thought, *Is that a good sign or a bad sign? I guess we will never know.* The D.A. and our attorney talked for a few minutes. If only I had been able to read their lips. The attorney came to us to say that we had been approved for a limited amount to pay the investigator and the psychologist. The amount given was not enough for both. We had to decide which one we needed the most. The attorneys and the D.A. finished, and we left.

I asked our attorney, "Are we are still going to trial?"

"Yes, we are still going to trial," she said.

She explained that the amount given for the psychologist was not enough. We might not have one unless we came up with some money to pay for one.

In the back of my mind I was thinking, *Are you kidding? We are trying to keep our house, the car has been repossessed, and we need money for a psychologist. Where are you, God? This is insane!*

"Do we have to have a psychologist?" I asked our attorney.

"Yes, we will need one to testify on our behalf."

I thought, *Oh my God, we are not going to win. My husband is going to prison!*

I needed to figure this out. Something had to happen for this stuff to go away. Maybe if I lost my mind or passed out, it would go away. This wasn't the first time I had thought about it. Then I prayed, "I need peace of mind. God, please give me peace!"

I would weep inside until my head hurt. I had to remember 1 Peter 5:7(KIV), which says, "Casting all your care upon him; for he careth for you." It was so hard to do when all hope seemed to be gone. I thought, *Well, if God cares, He will fix everything.*

Chapter 21

Being Content

Days went by, and the food in the house became scarce. The kids were content with whatever we had to eat. Then the next day, money would be in my account. It would be just enough to buy a few groceries to take us to payday. We tried to live our days as normally as possible. I dealt with the emotional strain of our kids and most of the time my husband. Sometimes at night he would just cry and ask why.

Life was not normal for us anymore. It was like life was here today and gone tomorrow. I could tell sometimes that my husband was afraid and trying not to show it because of the strong person he had tried to present for the previous nineteen years. No one is perfect, but overall, he was a good husband (something I had ignored). He was always a good father, and a good provider. My husband's upbringing taught him to take care of his family.

On September 20, we were in court, going through the process of preparing for the trial. We did not stay long. The court date was already set.

We did not have to return to court until the following month. Until then, my family and I did not really talk much about the trial. We just kept doing what we did every day. We were content because we couldn't do anything but go through this. Throughout this situation I went to work with a smile on my face, acting as if life was normal for me.

I talked with Mary Louise every day. She always encouraged my husband and me. She even took time out to talk with the kids.

Chapter 22

Signs of Doubt

Our financial situation was only getting worse. We were paying the attorneys every month. The co-attorney wanted my husband and me to drop by his office and discuss our financial situation. He was concerned about whether we would be able to pay him. We told him we were doing our best. Well, I guess our best was not good enough because later that day, our attorney said he wanted off the case because he was afraid we would not pay him. I did not feel bad because we did not want him anyway and had not asked for his service.

Our attorney was afraid because this was her first criminal case in this capacity, and she did not want to ruin an innocent man's life. We had faith in her that she would be fine, but I could tell she was very stressed about the case.

One day when the attorney came to the house to prepare for the trial, she and I had a chance to talk one-on-one. With a small amount of doubt in my mind, I asked her, "Do you think my husband did anything wrong?"

The attorney looked me straight in the eyes, long and hard, and said, "No. He did nothing wrong." That was the confirmation I needed for myself, deep down within my soul. That gift of discernment, realizing that my husband did nothing wrong, relaxed my mind. God had revealed many clues that I did not understand that proved his innocence.

Often, I wondered when this was going to be over. I would get a good feeling about it, but then reality would slap me with the thought that it could go the other way, turning for the worst. That is when I needed to pray to rebuild my faith. Matthew 17:20(KIV) says, "if I have the faith of a mustard seed," meaning I don't need a lot of faith, just a little.

Daily my faith increased. I listened to positive words from different ministries by television, attended a faith-based church, and listened to inspirational teaching on the radio. I began to read positive quotes and listen to many inspirational songs. Mary Louise and a few other friends would pray and talk about positive things with me.

A few days before court, our attorney called to tell us that the other attorney had decided to assist her with the trial. At this point, I did not care because as the official date for the trial drew closer, I began to feel low in spirit. But I would be all right because of the faith I continued to have.

On October 14, we went to court. The judge wanted us to come back so that they could start jury selection. She gave us a court date. When I heard the date, I thought to myself, *A jury! A real trial is about to take place. This is real, not a television show. A decision will be made that will determine our family's future.* We were amazed at how the criminal justice system could come into your life and turn it inside out. I had to keep faith.

On October 18, we were back in court, only this time, I had to sit in the lobby because they had to select the jury. I sat in the lobby trying to continue with my faith, but the thought of what was happening made me think the worst. Then I had to rebuild myself and the way I thought. I started speaking things as though they were already true. I started chanting to myself, "Dismiss, dismiss, dismiss." It made me feel better.

Chapter 23

The Trial

We did not invite my brothers-in-law or anyone else to the court because it was too embarrassing. We didn't want to burden anyone with our situation. We just asked people who knew to pray.

On October 24, the trial began. I was not allowed in the courtroom because I allowed my emotions to control me. While I was waiting, new information was revealed that was not in our favor. It was very upsetting, but I continued believing that everything was going to be all right.

On October 25, my children testified. Both children came out of the courtroom saying that they had told the truth. Telling the truth is something I raised my children to do. My husband and I would tell them to always be truthful; sometimes you might get in trouble, but you must tell the truth.

I hated that my children had to go through this. I was not allowed to testify because our attorney thought I would become hostile and cause a disaster in the trial. They thought my testimony would not help because I didn't know what had happened on August 26, 2009, in spite of being the first person to know about the allegations.

Chapter 24

Jury Deliberation –
"Angels in the Jury Room"

On October 26, the jury went to deliberate. We waited in the waiting room for them to reach a verdict. A friend, my two daughters, my husband, and I waited with contentment. I tried not to focus on the worst because I had finally accepted what God was going to allow. I thought about one of my favorite Scriptures, Deuteronomy 31:8 (NIV): "God will never leave me nor forsake me."

That day was an emotional day for me: it was the anniversary of the day my sweet mother-in-law died. I was thinking, *Her son is sitting, waiting to hear what his future holds.* As I continued to reflect, I noticed my husband had fallen into a deep sleep. Then all of a sudden, he woke up and started shouting, "There goes my mother, there goes my mother into the jury room. She is with another angel." We all looked at each other and didn't say anything. I finally asked him what he had seen. He explained that his mother and my mother had gone into the jury room. We just sat looking at him in astonishment. I suddenly realized that God had dispatched his angels from heaven.

Later, the attorney came to tell us to go home and that we would have to come back the next day because the jury couldn't make a decision. I wanted to pass out. I asked the attorney why. She said the fact that they couldn't make a decision was a good sign and could work in our favor. We left and went home for the evening.

After arriving home, we tried to have a normal evening, but the trial was still hanging over our heads. We called Mary Louise and spoke with her, and as always, she said, "Your husband is innocent." She told me I had to continue believing that God was going to work it out. After we finished our conversation, I went to bed and cried myself to sleep. I woke up with my husband chanting, "Thank you, Jesus. Thank you, Jesus." He told me everything was going to be all right, whichever way it went.

Around noon on October 27, the judge told the jury she was not feeding them another day and wanted to know their decision. The foreman got up and said, "We could not make a decision, Your Honor." Therefore, the judge declared a hung jury. The judge told my husband he was free to go, but a new trial could be re-filed.

After it was over, we went to the waiting room so that the attorney could explain what had just happened in the courtroom. She said that only two people believed the allegations weren't true. That meant the district attorney would probably try the case again, but at a later date. Our attorney felt good about the case. She said we would come back to court on December 21. I wanted to feel defeated, but I could not because my husband was coming home and not going to prison.

Chapter 25

Aftermath

We called our circle of friends who were praying for us, and they were excited about the outcome. They kept encouraging us that everything was going to be all right. I called Mary Louise and told her. She was very excited, so I guessed I needed to get excited too.

We enjoyed the Thanksgiving holiday by being thankful that some of the situation was over. Although the trial had not ended in our favor, we were still thankful.

In the early part of December, we received a call from our attorney saying she would no longer be our attorney.

We asked her why, and she said she felt too much stress from working on this type of case. We tried to persuade her to stay by encouraging her and even told her that the judge really liked her. But she had made her decision, so we needed another attorney.

On December 21, we were back in court. Our attorney and the co-attorney had both quit. The judge told my husband he would have to hire another attorney.

We went on to celebrate Christmas. In spite of what we were facing, we enjoyed the holiday season because we were together as a family. The kids and I did not have to visit my husband at a prison for the holidays. We did not have much to give to the kids, but they were grateful to have their father home with them.

As I reflected on the year, I thought to myself, *What an emotional year for me. Only God got me through this year. There were days I just wanted to die and leave this madness behind.* Then I thought, *I have so much to live for, in spite of all the chaos we are going through. But God has done this for me. God wants me to live to see what the end will be. The question is, "Will it end?"*

2012

Chapter 26

New Attitude

As always, we had our traditional dinner and celebrated Mary Louise's birthday on January 1. It was a bittersweet celebration because of the hung jury from the trial, with the possibility of a new trial and two new felony allegations pending. We made the best of the celebration. This was a nightmare happening to us, to me.

I promised myself this was the year everything was going to be all right. I was going to say only positive things. I was going to do positive things. I was going to just trust God.

The next court date was near, and we still didn't have an attorney and didn't have any money. I decided late one evening to contact a well-known attorney in the city. I called and spoke with the answering service and left a message. A few minutes later the phone rang, I answered, and on the line was that well-known attorney, returning my call. I was totally surprised to hear his voice. He was very kind to me and listened to my story. He instructed me to visit with his associate attorney. He said that once he returned from out of town, he wanted to talk with my husband and me.

After hanging up the phone, I just sat at the desk and started to cry. I thought about James 4:2 (NIV), which says, "You have not because you ask not." This Scripture teaches us how to ask God for what we need. Most of the time, we do not. We depend on our wisdom to fix our situation, but all we have to do is ask God.

The next day I made an appointment with the associate attorney, and my husband and I met with him a few days later.

He was already prepared to meet with us and had pulled the court record. He listened to our story, took notes, and asked us many questions about the case. In conclusion, he said that he would get the case dismissed but the cost would be eighty thousand dollars. My husband and I looked at each other and told him we did not have that kind of money. The associate said he understood and was willing to work with us. He reminded us that the well-known attorney wanted to meet with us and discuss our case. Before we left, my husband stepped out of the room, and while he was gone, I asked the associate his view on the case. He said that my husband was innocent and not to worry.

A few days later we met with the well-known attorney. He introduced himself to us and made us feel welcome. We went to his office for our meeting. The associate had already told him about our case. He began to ask my husband and me questions. He told us he believed my husband was innocent and he would get the case dismissed, but the cost would be a hundred thousand dollars. My husband asked if he could do it pro bono, but he said no. He also said the case should not have gone to trial because of the lack of evidence and the inconsistency of the allegations. He apologized that he was unable to represent us because of the lack of money. But he gave some good advice to my husband, telling him not to break down and take a plea bargain. He told him to fight the case because it did not make any sense.

We still did not have an attorney. We kept searching for one and trying to get one for the least money possible. This was a very expensive case, and no one was willing to take it for less than ten thousand dollars. I did my best not to give up. We needed to prepare for the next court date.

On January 17, we went to court without a hired attorney. My husband stood before the judge and said he had not hired an attorney yet. My husband told the judge that he had spoken with the well-known attorney, and she laughed out loud, saying, "You can't afford that attorney." She told my husband to hire an attorney because he would need one. Otherwise he could sit in jail and get a court-appointed attorney. The court date was reset.

Well, a financial crisis happened again: our only transportation broke down. We had to borrow a vehicle because we did not have the money to get our only vehicle fixed. My husband's friend told him to bring it to his shop, where he would work on it, as he got paid every other week. This was another expense we could not afford.

A few days later we hired an attorney. My husband met with him, and the attorney told him how much he was going to charge. The attorney's fee was so cheap that I got scared and knew my husband would go to prison. The old saying is that you get what you pay for. Although his fee was cheap, I had this epiphany that this was the attorney — this was the one. At least that's what I thought.

On January 25, my husband went back to court, this time without me. He went to court with a friend of ours. I went to the office and waited for him to call to tell me they had dismissed the case. The phone call I received from my husband was that the newly hired attorney had not shown up.

Well, we got through it. We did not understand it, but we also didn't realize God was in this. I thought to myself, *What is next?*

Chapter 27

New Arrest

While I was at work four days later, my husband called around noon. He said he was being arrested on the two new charges and was on his way to jail. He was doing just fine, though, and was not upset. As he was talking, I walked into my office manager's office and closed the door. While talking to my husband, I was telling her what was going on. For the strangest reason, I did not panic, I did not cry, but remained calm. He said the police officer wanted to speak with me. I thought, *That's strange.* "Hello?"

"Everything is okay," the officer said. "We are just doing what we are supposed to do."

"I understand."

"Your husband did nothing, and this is what I want you to do. I am going to hold him at the police station; you call your bonding company and make arrangements to pick him up here today."

He kept saying, "Everything is going to be all right. Don't worry." He also said, "I have seen this type of case many times, and I know your husband has done nothing wrong."

I kept thinking to myself, *This is so amazing that people with whom I come in contact keep telling me that my husband did nothing wrong.* That was what I needed to hear to help me keep fighting on his behalf. It still amazed me that I was part of the criminal justice system but also a victim of the system.

The timing of the arrest was of the essence. First I did not have any money to bail my husband out, but God had this time set perfectly. All of this happened one day before my payday. I called the bonding company and asked if I could give them a postdated check, and they immediately said yes. That is why it is so important to ask. Recalling one of my favorite Scriptures, "You have not because you ask not."

I had to call my oldest daughter to pick me up at the office. She was about twenty minutes away. In the meantime, I called Mary Louise and told her what was going on. She was concerned about my mental state and asked if I was going to be okay. I told her not to worry, I was doing just fine and my daughter was on her way to pick me up.

My daughter arrived and I told my office manager I was leaving. She said, "Go and take care of your business and get your husband out of jail." I made a smooth exit out of the building without anyone noticing me leaving early.

While I was driving, I told my daughter what was going on, and she was very calm. I told her that this couldn't get any worse than it already was. I started to really reflect while driving to the bonding company. My investigative mind was working. I told my daughter, "I need to know the dates these incidents supposedly occurred." I kept repeating, "I need to know the dates." Then I begin to get sad. I thought, *My poor husband is going through this stuff and it is unfair.* I had to keep a happy face on in front of my daughter. I did not want her to see me sad. I turned my face to the window and wiped away a tear.

I called Mary Louise, and she just could not believe what was happening. She started to pray, asking God to bring this situation to a close. I told her I would keep her posted on what was going on.

I arrived at the bonding company, and they had all the paperwork ready for me to sign. They said for me not to worry, that everything was going to be all right. They also said my husband was a good customer and they didn't have a problem with helping him out. Hearing all that really put a smile on my face, and I got a good feeling that everything was going to be all right.

We left the bonding company and headed to the city jail. This was my first time making this type of transaction at the city jail. I spoke to the jailer; she said the district attorney had not processed the paperwork for the new charges. She said it would take a while and to check back later. It was already three o'clock in the afternoon. My oldest daughter and I waited for hours, until it was time to get dinner. I called the jail to check the status, but nothing had changed yet. We drove back to our parking spot and waited some more. About two hours later I checked the city jail again, and this time my husband was ready to be released.

My husband walked out of the door coming from the holding tank. My eyes caught his true emotion, and it became obvious that he was very upset. I noticed he had on some slippers that they had given him to wear while in jail.

He came and sat next to me on the bench and changed back into his work boots. He picked the slippers up off the floor and angrily dumped them in the trash can outside the exit doors. I hesitated to ask him if he was okay, but I finally got up the nerve to ask.

He replied bitterly, "I am just tired of the interruption and the humiliation."

I became somewhat nervous.

Then he shouted, "The police came to my job and picked me up. I have not done anything wrong. I have not done anything wrong."

My oldest daughter began to cry, expressing the hurt she felt for her dad.

In a quiet voice I said to both of them, "Everything is going to be all right. I believe that."

Chapter 28

Essence of Time

After leaving the jail my husband had to go to the bonding company to check in. I told him to ask the bonding clerk the dates of the new allegations. My daughter and I sat in our borrowed vehicle and waited. About twenty minutes later he came back to the vehicle and I asked him what the dates were. My daughter recognized them immediately.

We finally arrived home, and I rushed into the house and got on the computer to check the dates of my husband's military travel. We discovered that my husband had not been in the city or even in the country on the dates of the allegations. I became upset once I discovered this travel information. I thought, *Oh my God, what is going on?* Then I said out loud, "God, what are you doing?"

Chapter 29

Bad News

Later in February, Mary Louise called me with bad news, saying that her cancer had come back. I was speechless. I pulled the phone away from my face and begin to cry. All I could think was *Who will listen to me and pray with me like Mary Louise?* I became selfish. Now it was her turn to have me listen to her and pray with her. How could this be happening now, when all this mess was going on with me?

Mary Louise had known me since I was in high school. She was the supporter of my family, but now she was sick again. What was I to do now? I refused to imagine being without her.

After regaining my composure, I told her, "You will be fine."

Chapter 30

Do Not Depend on Man

February 21, was another court date. Our friend was going to be there with us again. I really believed that a dismissal would come soon. Although we were told that we would go through another trial, I was convinced that God would see us through and the case would get dismissed. This time in court it was about the same. The district attorney still wanted to go to trial again but asked if my husband would take a plea bargain. Our attorney already knew the answer was no. The court date was reset.

Our friend decided to end his financial obligation to us based on a decision that did not make any sense to us. It was well appreciated, but the way it ended hurt. But God knew the reason behind his decision. It seemed like a setback, but God had a better comeback for us. It was disappointing that although our friend questioned the reason why, the answer just didn't make any sense. We still continued to move forward. We did not stop. It was a lesson for us not to depend on man but to depend on God.

Chapter 31

More Interesting Changes and a Miracle

On March 2, while driving to court, I told my husband I would not be surprised if they had changed judges. He said, "Yeah that really would be something."

We arrived at the courthouse. I dropped my husband off because I needed to go to my office. Our oldest daughter was meeting him at the courthouse so he would have a ride home.

I arrived at my office and began to work on a few things that were pending. As I was working, my mind was thinking about my husband at court and wondering what was going on. I would start my chant of "Dismiss" but would become nervous because I was not there. I knew God was with him, but I should have stayed with him, I thought. I noticed that I did not have peace of mind, so I began to pray silently for peace. God gave me peace. While I was working hard and being productive at work, I finally got the call from my husband. "Guess what," he said.

"What? Dismiss?"

"Not that," he said. "They changed judges."

I sat back in my chair with my mouth wide open. "Do you remember me talking about that this morning?"

"Yep" He went on to say, "The worst thing about changing to another judge is that now I have to report to pretrial community supervision every time I go to court, and take a urine test."

"What? That is an insult." I became angry. I thought, *This is ridiculous and unfair.*

My husband said the reason for the change was that he was military and the judge handled all military cases. That was the procedure in his court. I didn't want to accept the change, but I had no choice.

I said, "That is dumb."

God heard my statement that morning and knew the plan, so I had to watch God do what He was going to do. The transcript from the previous trial was going to cost us about four thousand dollars or more, but God gave it to us free. I had been worried about how we were going to pay for the transcript, but Matthew 6:31–32 says, "Therefore do not be anxious, saying, 'What shall we eat?' or 'What shall we drink?' or 'What shall we wear?' For the Gentiles seek after all these things, and your heavenly Father knows that you need them all." God knew we needed that transcript and needed it for free. That was what God was trying to show me: that He had this.

Although the other two cases were added, we were well convinced now that God was already ahead of us. I was comfortable enough now to say, "So what, he has three cases against him." The court date was reset.

March 2, was a sentimental day for me. It was the day my mother had died twenty-three years previously. It was a crazy, strange day. I believe an angel was dispatched from heaven again to make things better.

In March I was obligated to an organization, and I looked forward to it every year. It was my happy time. I didn't schedule or plan anything during this time. The best part of the month was the birth of my first baby in 1991. I loved the month of March.

On April 3, we were in court. Going to court had become routine. I had adjusted to going every month. I would take vacation time from my job; it was a part of our lives now. It felt like a lifetime commitment, but Psalm 23 says, "as we go through …," which meant that we had to come out of the situation; there would be an end to it.

While we were sitting in court, the district attorney did not show. I thought, *Well, that is not a good sign, but I am still open to hearing "Dismissed."* All we got was another court reset.

A few days later we were faced with a traumatic experience with Mary Louise. She went through surgery successfully, experiencing Psalm 23:4, which says, "Yea though I walk through the valley of the shadow of death …"

Chapter 32

Depression

April 14 was my fiftieth birthday. I could not celebrate because I did not feel like it. I experienced a deep depression. I felt like closing my eyes forever. I stayed in my bed all day. I did not want to be bothered with anyone. My son came to the room, lay down beside me on the bed, and said innocently, "Mama, you are getting old, but I love you."

In the middle of the day one of my cousins came and dropped off balloons, a card, and some money. I laid back down and just cried. I guess the pressure of dealing with the situation of the previous four years finally got the best of me.

I was not sure if I could come out of this depression. It was my secret at the time. I did not tell anyone about how I was feeling. Mary Louise was recovering from her surgery. Jenny had her own issues, so I had no one else to depend on, not even my family. I had to get it together. I felt helpless because my mother died over 23 years ago. I did not want to talk to anyone. As I lay in my bed, I reflected on all the blessings God had granted my family and me, and then I went to sleep.

By daybreak God had pulled me out of that deep depression. My husband and children needed me. I was a stronger person. I had to get up and move forward.

Deuteronomy 31:8 (NIV) says, "The Lord himself goes before you and will be with you; he will never leave you nor forsake you. Do not be afraid; do not be discouraged."

Chapter 33

A Trip Overseas

May 3 was another court date. In court this time, our attorney was trying to get certain motions and the list of the jurors from the previous trial. I was really feeling that everyone involved in the courtroom knew this case was a waste of time. I was thinking, *Reset after reset. When is it going to come to an end?* One good thing did come out of all of this: my husband got the approval to take one last trip out of the country before he retired from the military on June 1. That was an indication that the judge knew my husband was not a threat to society and was an innocent man. This type of case has very strict orders. But the judge granted his approval to travel. God really showed us favors. The court date was reset.

As the month of May moved forward, many good things were happening in our favor. My husband traveled overseas and returned home safely. The burden of our situation was becoming lighter. Often we say that we have given our problems to God, but we still take them back and try to fix them ourselves. This causes a delay to our blessing. We must be patient and trust Him.

Mary Louise was coming along quite well since her surgery. We talked daily. I tried not to burden her with the situation, but she wanted to be updated every time we went to court.

On June 1, after 22 years my husband officially retired from the military. This was one of his goals. I began to reflect that day how my husband had been looking forward to retiring, which was another reason I believed he would not have committed a crime. This retirement was very important to him. June was a good month for me because my second daughter was born on June 2, 1998.

On June 6, we were back in court. There was nothing new happening; it was the same process of going to court every month. We just made ourselves content. My husband was also reporting back from his military overseas trip. More motions were filed. Court was reset for two weeks later. A lot of weird things were starting to happen. I didn't want to get my hopes up, but I really began to have faith that everything was going to work out on our behalf.

Chapter 34

Another District Attorney

The district attorney said they were ready for trial, and our attorney said he was ready for trial as well. I was emotionally drained. I stopped trying to feel this way and that way. I was giving everything totally to God. I was even saying, "Whatever your will is, let it be done." My faith was increasing. God had shown us many signs that everything was going to be all right.

On June 18, we were back in court. I did not understand why we were beginning to go to court twice a month. I felt like something was going on but could not figure it out. While sitting in the courtroom, we did not see the district attorney. There were other attorneys and district attorneys there, but I did not see the one for our case. Our attorney walked toward us and said, "Let's go." I was confused. We went to the waiting room, and our attorney said they had changed district attorneys. I asked why. He said they were bouncing our case around because nobody wanted to take it because it didn't seem likely to win. I thought in my mind, *The state is just wasting our time, but the other motive is to see if my husband will give in and take a plea bargain.* Our attorney had already met with the new district attorney, and the first thing out of her mouth was a plea bargain. He immediately told her no because, he said, his client had not done anything wrong. That is why we had come back sooner than we needed to. They set a pretrial date and a date for the trial. This would also give the new district attorney time to gather her facts. I thought, *get your facts and convince me that my husband has committed a crime.*

During the rest of the month, God was working in our favor and we could see the miracles He was bringing into our lives. One of the major miracles was our mortgage payment. We hadn't made a payment for almost a year. I kept getting approval for loan modifications, which was my way of getting the payments delayed until we had the money to make one. This time a modification was not approved and our home was put on the foreclosure list to be sold in July.

A few days later I received a call from the bank asking if we wanted to stay in our home. I immediately told them yes. They invited my husband and me to meet with a loan officer on a certain date. We needed to bring all the necessary documents such as pay stubs, tax information, and utility bills to their office.

We went to their office and talked with a loan officer. Then we waited. An hour went by before another loan officer called us to his office. We sat down, and the first thing I asked was "Are you all able to help us keep our house?"

The loan officer replied, "Yes." He gathered all the printed documents and explained each one. "Your interest rate has dropped two points, your payment is lower, and you will make the first payment November 1, 2012." It was another favor from God. The income my husband made from his trip allowed us to be put ahead in order for us to make the first payment in November.

On July 23, we were back in court again. It was redundant, but we had to do what we were ordered to do. Our attorney and the district attorney said a few words. I noticed that our attorney had an angry expression on his face, but he kept his cool. He walked toward us and pointed to the door. My husband and I walked behind him to the same meeting room, and he told us we were going to fight this case to the end.

He looked at my husband and said, "You are not taking a plea bargain and you are not going to prison." We did not ask our attorney what had been said that made him upset; we just accepted what he said, and we all left the room. Our attorney told us he would talk to us later, and we went our separate ways. My husband and I rode the elevator down without saying a word to each other. I felt somewhat confused because of how our meeting with the attorney had concluded, but I had a good feeling too.

Chapter 35

A Stronger Faith

We kept our focus on God. Deuteronomy 31:6 (NIV) says, "Be strong and courageous. Do not be afraid or terrified because of them, for the Lord your God goes with you; he will never leave you nor forsake you." This is what I lived by: that God would not forsake us. I did not know everything God was doing when we went to court. Although it had taken me a while to accept what God was allowing, I knew He had a plan. I even felt like the many songs on the radio would play as if the DJ knew what I was going through. The song would encourage me to the point where I began to really believe it when I said, "Dismiss."

My husband's truck was ready to be picked up. The mechanic gave him a payment plan to follow instead of having him pay the full amount at once. This was another one of God's favors.

While getting closer to the next court date, my mind began to drift into negative thoughts. After all the many blessings and favors God had given us.

I still had moments of negative thoughts. I had to remember that I had to keep my mind together because I had to stay focused to help keep everyone else focused. There were times when my husband would go into a deep depression because of the hurt he was experiencing. I would have to talk him through it along with the medication he was given for his depression. Then there were times when he would become angry, saying that he had tried to do everything right but still failed. Not to mention my children: I did not want them to lose focus as well. Again, those were the reasons I had to stay focused.

On August 20, we were in court. My husband was late for the first time. The docket was called at 8:30 a.m. and my husband got there at 8:55 a.m. He was told he would be put in jail if he couldn't get to court on time. He did not respond; he just put his head down. I sat next to him, wondering what he was thinking while waiting for his attorney to arrive. I touched his hand and whispered, "Are you all right?" He nodded yes. I could see the disappointment and the frustration in his face. I could tell he was tired of coming to court. Our attorney arrived, spoke to us, talked to the district attorney, walked over to the clerk, and walked toward us while pointing to the door. We left. It was another wasted morning. Court was reset again.

As the time passed by, I began to reflect on the struggle of our situation. I was thinking about what I could have done to prevent these allegations against my husband. Then I thought about Romans 8:28 (NIV): "And we know that in all things God works for the good of those who love him, who have been called according to his purpose." Then I begin to think about how my husband and I love God and that He had a purpose for everything that happened in our lives. We don't understand, but we have to keep trusting and believing that all things work together, whether good or bad.

It was school time for the kids, and we had to decide whether to buy school clothes or pay the utility bill. I called the utility company again, asking for an extension on the bill. For the last few months, they had denied my request for an extension. I would have to do a payday load to get the bill paid, and I used whatever I had left over to buy groceries.

This time I asked for an extension again. They transferred me to a supervisor. I explained briefly what was going on with our finances, they put me on hold for a few minutes, and they came back on the line and asked when I could pay the bill.

Tears begin to well up in my eyes. I told them when I could pay and the person told me to hold again. I waited a few more minutes until the person came back on the line and said, "We will give you until that date to pay your bill." I was speechless and began to weep silently. I told the person that God was going to truly bless them for blessing me. I told them my mother had sent me an angel. The person laughed and asked if they could help me with anything else. "You have helped me enough," I said. "Thank you, and have a good evening." Again, we have not because we ask not. That is why I ask. I was able to get the kids a new pair of sneakers, a backpack, and uniforms to start the first week of school. God had granted me another favor.

Chapter 36

Another Plea Bargain

September 24 was court time again. It was another court reset. Nothing had changed; the process was the same. I was thinking I might just go to the office. Then I thought, *This is another day of vacation.* My husband and I just went to lunch.

I thought I was doing pretty well mentally, making sure everyone remained positive. I also confined with another friend from work, Greta who helped me understand things not from an emotional but a legal point of view. On some days I would try not to talk to her, but she would always sense when I needed to talk. I hated to hear her say that this case was going to take a long time. She would end by saying, "I will pray for you all." That was the best thing to do because we know that prayer changes things.

It was getting closer to another day in court. This time I was looking for something to happen. I started chanting "Dismiss" early, a few days before court. I believed that God would hear me and grant it to me this time.

They were talking so deeply, I said, "This is it" silently. My husband was sitting beside me looking unconcerned. I wanted to tell him this was it, but I could not say anything except to myself: this is it.

On October 15, we were in court again. I knew God

was going to do it this time. I felt it in my bones. We watched our attorney having a deep conversation with the district attorney. I was doing my chant in my mind: *Dismiss, dismiss.* Then I was reading our attorney's lips. He was saying, "No, no, no." I noticed the district attorney gathering her briefcase

and both attorneys walking over to the clerk's desk. Then our attorney walked past us, pointing to the door. We got up quickly to catch him. He went to the waiting room, where he paced the floor. I asked what had happened. He said the state wanted to make a deal, which explained why he was saying no. My husband said, "What deal?" Our attorney said they had offered seven years' probation and to dismiss the other two cases. He said he had told the state, "No, hell, no!"

My husband said, "But I did nothing wrong. Why are they trying to get me to admit to something I did not do?"

I said, "It's their job to win, but this time they will not win." Instead of getting angry I got this amazing feeling that we would win. I didn't know when it was going to happen, but it was going to happen. I thanked our attorney for all the effort he was putting toward helping us.

While driving home, my husband said, "If I had done something wrong, I wouldn't have taken you and the kids through this. I would have taken a plea bargain from the beginning. I wouldn't have given my money to an attorney. I would have given my 401(k) to you so that you could take care of yourself and the children. You could have moved on with your lives. I love my family too much to have kept this going. I haven't done anything to anyone. I am so tired, but I must fight."

As we continued driving home, I reflect on the fact that while I was growing up, I was told to stand for the truth. I looked over at him and he had tears rolling down his face, and it made me weep. I had never seen my husband this low after a court date.

This month was the anniversary of my mother-in-law's death. It had been already three years. As I reflected during this time, I became sad because after her death, my children were taken from me and they missed their grandmother's funeral. It was hard to start the healing process because I thought about how she had died without knowing what was going on with her son, my husband.

Chapter 37

The Last Holiday

The holiday season was approaching, and we still had another court date. We made the best of our Thanksgiving by being thankful. Although the year had had many roadblocks, we had gotten through them. As we were reflecting, we were thankful that we were all still together.

On November 26, we were in court again. Ten years earlier on that date, I had given birth to our son. He was the best thing that could have happened to us, and the first boy in my family. The district attorney said that if we went to trial, the state would ask for twenty years in prison. I thought boldly, *Okay, bring it on.* For the weirdest reason I was not intimidated. My husband said, "Well, if I get twenty years for the truth, so be it." The court did not kill our spirit. We would not have to come back in December. We walked out of the courtroom happy. It was still a good day. The court date was reset.

The month of December changed our lives forever. I finally decided to tell my dear friend Sherry what we were going through. Sherry and her husband opened their arms of support to my family. Their church invited my youngest daughter to sing at their Christmas event. My daughter sang so well that Sherry suggested that the music department have a concert featuring my daughter. I thought *Okay* without any concern about the event. I thought to myself, *this is too much to do for my daughter.* Sherry had a vision, and my daughter was part of her vision.

Later in the month I encountered a coincidental moment in my life. I met a lady I had never met before. She told me that she worked for Child Protective Services. I was amazed and needed to ask her a few questions.

I began to tell her about a friend of mine (the friend was me), and she began to tell me what my friend needed to do. Then I broke down and told her that the "friend" was me. She said, "That's okay; I figured it was you." As I went to tell her about my children being removed from my home back in 2009, she interrupted me. She asked, "Were the children a boy and a girl?" I said yes. Then she said, "Were they trying to go to their grandmother's funeral?"

I said yes. "How did you know?"

She said, "I trained the caseworker." I just looked at her in amazement. I told her that the kids hadn't gone to the funeral and that they were taken from me. She put a hand to her face, and her eyes welled up with tears. We just both looked at each other for a minute without saying anything. She finally said in a low voice that the kids were supposed to go to their grandmother's funeral and the case was supposed to be closed because of lack of evidence and because the stories were not consistent.

After we finished our conversation and went our separate way, my thoughts about our case totally changed. My eyes were opened to a new way of looking at our case. I began to process all of this in my mind and recognize that everything was going to be all right. This was very important information to share with our attorney.

I contacted our attorney and told him about the information I had just received. He said that this was good information and he knew what to do with it.

Although we didn't know what we would be facing in the New Year, we enjoyed the Christmas holidays with our family. The kids didn't get all they wanted for Christmas, but they were happy that we were all together. They also knew that Jesus was the reason for the season.

As the year closed, I reminisced about how all the blessings and favors outweighed the negative things that were going on. We went from almost losing our home to making a payment every other week without a problem. We had food on the table, and we were healthy. Mary Louise had had surgery, and God had brought her out well. I had survived without totally breaking down mentally because of our family and friends, who surrounded us with support and love. I had met some amazing people who had helped us through this life-changing experience.

I thought about my mother and how strong she was. Then I said, *I am just like my mother: a strong woman.*

2013

Chapter 38

Content with the State in Our Lives

January 1, brought another year and another celebration as we continued the tradition. We celebrated Mary Louise's birthday along with our traditional dinner. We didn't have many friends over this time, but we cooked the same menu, ate, and enjoyed the day.

My family and I were going into the fifth year of being tied down to the state. It had become a component of our lives. I began to look forward to going to court every month. I would not schedule anything on our court date. I did not hesitate to schedule a vacation day from my job every month. I stopped worrying about saving my vacation. Even the kids had adjusted to our going to court; they stopped asking what had happened in court when we returned home. I did know that it would come to an end because 1 Corinthian 10:13 says that "God does not put more on you than you can bear." I really believe this Scripture.

We were at home one evening when someone knocked on the front door. I opened the door and Sherry burst through, demanding that I get a calendar to plan my daughter's concert at her church. I honestly didn't feel like planning.

Sherry, my daughter, and I sat at the table going

through the calendar to set a date for the concert. When I noticed the smile on my daughter's face, I began to feel excited about planning it. Sherry began to explain to us why it was important to have this concert. She said God had given her a vision about it. We set a date and began to plan.

Although we were planning the concert, we still had court ahead of us. We still didn't know what was in our future. I had to shift my focus. I had no control over what was happening in my family. I knew that God was in control. I had seen many indications that everything was going to be all right, but doubt was having a field day with my mind.

On January 28, we went to court. As we sat in court waiting to see what was going to happen, I noticed our attorney and the district attorney seeming to enjoy their conversation. I was thinking to myself, *What's so funny?* I became somewhat upset because I just wanted this stuff over with, and they were laughing. Then I started thinking, *God is in control.*

Our attorney walked over to the clerk's desk, walked by us, and pointed to the door. We went to our usual spot in the waiting room, and our attorney informed us that the district attorney was getting married and was not able to have the trial until after the wedding in May. I asked him why they couldn't just dismiss this stuff. Our attorney said that everything was going to be okay. We went our separate ways.

I left the courthouse very disappointed. I noticed that the expression on my husband's face was very calm. I thought to myself, *so why am I upset?* I began to change my thoughts and say positive things. We began to talk about our daughter's concert and what we were going to cook for dinner. I stopped worrying about what had happened in court and got excited because we didn't have to be back until June. I could accumulate some vacation time for the next few months. Only God knew our future.

In the month of February, I continued planning the concert and inviting guests. I really started to enjoy the planning. Everyone I invited to the concert said yes to the invitation. It was almost time for my favorite part of the year. I was in an organization that held a fund-raising event for a scholarship. It starts off with a barbecue cook-off and then the big event in March.

February 20, was my late mother's birthday. She would have been eighty years old. As I think back about her, I just smile. My mother was a lady of distinction. She was a God-fearing woman. She would trust God for everything. I heard her say that one day she was going to get a Cadillac. Not long after that, my dad purchased my mother a Cadillac. When she wanted to travel anywhere, she would just go. Her faith was very strong until her death. After all I had dealt with in the last five years, again I could proudly say that I am just like my mother.

March was a good month. I was doing my annual volunteer work. I had a blast. It made me feel really good. I saw an old friend from the previous year. Along with all the fun I was having, I was still planning the concert. It was coming along very well.

Later in the month Mary Louise's illness took a turn for the worse. We were not talking every day like usual. I didn't know what to do. Jenny was there, but I needed Mary Louise too.

I would call and speak with her husband once a week to check on her. He began to encourage my family and me. He would say, "I know when you all go to trial again, your husband will be all right." I really began to believe it!

Chapter 39

The Concert and a Financial Restoration

At four o'clock April 7, another experience began. My second daughter, fourteen years old, had her first gospel concert. The church was full and everything was excellent. With the help of God the concert was a blessing to many as well as to my daughter and our family. The pastor and his wife along with the church family changed my daughter's life forever. One of her guest, professional recording artist, J. Shep, was mesmerized by her singing and dedicated his time, service, and mentorship to her singing career. The church gave my daughter a financial start to her singing career.

As we started to connect with the J. Shep and his family, it added flavor to what God had planned for us. His music would be the highlight of our lives. He gave my daughter an opportunity that changed her life.

At this point, that was the only thing holding my head up!

In May, the J. Shep wrote and produced a song that kept me focused. The J. Shep's CD would take my way of thinking to a new level. The song "Let Go" was the featured song, but the song "I Can Depend on You" was the one I would play to make me feel that God was right next to me and guiding me through my difficult time. It reminded me of the Scripture that says, "He will never leave me nor forsake me."(Hebrews 13:5 KJV)

The mentor had a debut concert in the month of May for his newly released CD. He invited my daughter to sing. The audience adored her singing and applauded quite a bit. After the concert she was lavished with praise about her singing, and it made her feel good.

As I watched and observed the excitement my daughter was experiencing, it felt like it was just another sign that everything was going to be all right.

Days went by before it was time to go to court. I was waiting for God to bless me with a car. I put in my mind the type of car I wanted, and stuck with it. One of my friends said to me one day, "They have 2012 vehicles really cheap." I thought about it, and then said to myself, *I want that 2013.*

My husband was waiting on the approval of his military benefits. One day at home, I noticed that a brown envelope had been on the table for about three days. It was addressed to my husband from Washington, DC. I gave it to him, he opened it, and our lives changed. We had had the blessing sitting on the table for three days and hadn't even realized it.

God restored our finances in His time. We had many days of not having the things we needed and wanted because of money spent on legal fees. Matthew 6:33 says, "But seek first the kingdom of God and his righteousness, and all these things will be added to you." It is very important to seek God and be faithful because God keeps His promises.

A few days before court, my daughter had to sing out of town. I reserved a small vehicle for us to rent for the trip. I had a desire to rent my favorite car. While waiting for the reservationist to finish the rental process, she asked, "Where are you all going?" I shared with her that my daughter was going to sing. I played a song of my daughter singing for her, and while she was listening, she was spiritually touched and upgraded my rental to my favorite car and the same car I wanted to own. This was a sign that everything was going to be all right and that God was in control of everything.

On our way back from our trip, I was talking to a car salesman. He was trying to approve us for a car. We had been turned down many times by other car dealers before, especially for the car I wanted.

This particular salesman was determined to get us approved for a car. He called me with an approval for different cars other than the one I wanted. I was excited about the approval, but he couldn't get us approval for the car I wanted. At this point I began to think I would just settle for any car. We had been without air-conditioning in the one vehicle for the previous two years. I was eager just to get anything at this point. Then the Scripture came to mind about not being too anxious for nothing (Philippians 4:6–7).

I began to pray and tell God, "This car I am driving: I want to drive it to the car dealer, and return it to the rental in my new car." This was my prayer.

While driving I was listening to a song called "Haven't Forgot" from J. Shep's CD. As the song played, it begin to minister to me, assuring me that God had not forgotten me and not to be afraid. I began to weep silently and sing along with the song. I kept saying to myself, *God has not forgotten me over* and over again. I kept repeating it even after the song was over. The moment was broken by the phone ringing. It was the car salesman telling me that he had gotten us approval for the car I wanted. My husband had said that if we got a car, he wanted a white one.

I asked the salesman, "What color is it?"

"White," he said.

At this point I just wanted to stop the car on the side of the road and start shouting. I kept driving with tears rolling down my face like a never-ending river. I called my husband to tell him the good news. He was very excited.

God granted my prayer. I picked up my new car, my husband drove the rental back to the rental company, and we drove away from the rental company in the new car I had asked God for.

After God granted this prayer, I began to totally believe that He was going to bring us out of our situation victoriously. The Sunday before our next court date I heard a sermon that said God was going to fix that legal issue you have been dealing with for a while. I could not believe what I was hearing and began to cry. This really increased my faith even more. I didn't know what was going to happen in court the next day, but my faith was stronger than before. I felt a pressure release from me. I felt light and it was a virtuous feeling. I had never felt that way before.

Chapter 40

The Dream and a Vacation

On June 17, we went back to court. This time felt very different. I did not feel afraid while I watched the action in the courtroom. When the attorney arrived, I was glad to see him. His face looked different, just like everything else seemed different from the other times we had been to court.

The attorney approached us and said we had a trial date set. After hearing those words, I began to experience this undeniably present feeling that sent my blood racing through my body. The thought of the case receiving a not-guilty verdict was uncomfortably refreshing. I was afraid to accept the fact that going to the courtroom every month was about to be over. Just as I began to enjoy the thought of it all being over and the rush it gave me, doubt hit me harder than I could ever have expected. I hadn't felt a feeling like this before. It sent a cold sweat down my spine. I needed to quickly catch myself, so I thought about 2 Timothy 1:7, which is about the spirit of fear. Then a strong feeling came upon me and took away my uncertainty. At that moment I regained the feeling that this was going to be over and would end in our favor.

I thought about the story of Peter stepping out of the boat to walk on the water to Jesus. He had faith that he could walk on water until doubt came to him and he began to sink, crying, "Jesus, save me." Jesus saved Peter from drowning.

That is what was revealed to me: that Jesus would save us from drowning in the justice system. Yes, I was ready for the trial.

My husband said we needed this to be over so we could move on with our lives. We left the courtroom feeling at peace.

It appeared that Mary Louise was not going to recover from her illness. I had a dream about her one night. She was sitting in a room looking as if she were waiting for someone. I saw her getting happy when we told her the trial was over and it had ended in our favor. Then she sat back in her chair and closed her eyes, never to open them again. I woke up and wanted to cry. Instead I began to pray, saying, "Please, God, don't take her from me. Please heal her body."

My husband sent the two younger kids and me on a trip to Baltimore, with all expenses paid plus spending money for an annual church convention. It was a much-needed trip for us. We had the best time of our lives. My daughter was able to perform with the orchestra during the convention.

One day while waiting for my daughter to finish rehearsal, we met a wonderful young lady who was the public relations person for the convention. I began to share with her about my youngest daughter's musical gifts, and she said she would like to do an interview with her. When my daughter arrived, I introduced them, and the young lady did a five-minute interview with her. This was a blessing to my daughter, and one of the highlights of our trip.

Chapter 41

The Last Trial

As the court date approached, our attorney called and said he needed to meet with the family to prepare us and wanted to have a female co-attorney to assist him during the trial.

A few days before the trial, we met with the attorney. He explained that they needed to select the jury on the first day and the trial would begin the next day. He told my husband not to be afraid, that he knew he didn't commit any crime, and to answer all the questions as accurately as possible. He told my son and my youngest daughter to tell the truth. Then he said to me, "You get to finally tell your side of the story."

As the days moved closer to the trial date, I continued to feel good about life. The shift in my feelings about these circumstances gave me a burst of energy. The friends who knew about our case called with encouraging words, and some of them wanted to come to court. My husband and I agreed that we didn't want anyone to come to the court, not even his own family. We just asked everyone to pray.

My husband got up early on July 29, the first day of court, and we prayed. We all got in the car and drove toward the courthouse.

As we were driving, we read our favorite Scripture, Psalm 31. This book of Psalms was written for the chief musician but was meant for the chief musician who was involved in this case.

We arrived at the courthouse on time. My husband had to go directly to the courtroom for the jury selection. The kids and I waited in the waiting room until the jury selection was completed. The trial began. I began to feel somewhat depressed because I got caught up in my emotions. I began to pray and rely on my faith to take the depression away. I had to remain strong for my family.

When court adjourned for the day, we met in the waiting room with our attorneys to debrief. Our attorney said it had been a good day. He said he felt good about everything.

We left the courthouse for the day. We could not foresee what was in store, but the atmosphere surrounding my family was very positive. We got home with the same positive atmosphere and routine for the evening, and prepared ourselves for the next day.

On July 30, day two, we convened back at court. The two younger kids and I could not be in the courtroom during the trial because we had to testify. My oldest daughter was able to be in the courtroom. The day was going by very slowly.

We sat in the waiting room without talking. This was not a good idea because my mind wanted to drift to thinking the worst. Still, I could feel the prayers of the righteous in the atmosphere. I would think about how much faith I have and how in the end we would win.

A few attorney friends stopped by the waiting room. One was going to testify, and the other came for support. It was an extraordinary day because it was full of laughter. When court was adjourned for the day, the attorneys came for the debriefing and said they still felt positive about the case.

Although we had had a day full of laughter and the attorneys feeling positive, I started to feel dejected, but the prayers surrounding us made me feel content.

That day was my husband's birthday. He was sitting in court not knowing if this would be his last birthday as a free man. Later that evening we celebrated his birthday. We did laugh, saying, "What a way to celebrate a birthday." We all watched some TV, prayed, and prepared for the next day.

On July 31, day three, we convened back in court, doing the same routine. This was going to be a short day. It was the day my husband got to tell what he was told he was accused of doing. This felony allegation could put him in prison for the rest of his life.

The judge had to leave early that day, and by the time court was adjourned, I was at peace with the day's outcome.

Later that afternoon, I needed to go to my office to try to complete some work because I had been out for court. My husband and I were riding to the office when the phone rang. It was my youngest daughter. She revealed a very dark secret that she just could not hold on to any longer. What she revealed justified her abnormal behavior. I became down in spirit. I almost couldn't go to the office to do any work. This was an emotional setback for me. I immediately called our attorney for instruction on how to handle this outcry from my own child. After discussing this new development, the attorney asked us to invite some family and friends to come to court in support of my husband.

I called a few people and invited them to court, and my husband called his oldest brother and invited him. Everyone we called committed to being in court the next day.

August 1, was the final day of testimony. The family and friends we had invited were in court with my husband. We were surprised to see one friend with whom I had never discussed our legal issue.

I was still feeling the emotional disaster from the new investigation that needed to be conducted. This was the day the kids and I were to testify.

Before going in, my son said to me, "Mama, I can't wait to testify. They need to know the truth and that my daddy didn't do anything wrong to anybody."

"Just tell the truth," I told him. My son testified and did extremely well. When he was brought back to the waiting room, the co-attorney commended my son for doing a good job.

Then it was time for my youngest daughter to testify. She seemed a little uptight and nervous, but I knew she would tell the truth and reveal her dark secret. She was the only one who could truly shine light on what she had had to deal with for a long time. I could only imagine how tired she was, along with the rest of us. She just wanted to tell the truth and get it over with, and she did.

Then it was my turn to finally tell the other side of the story. I was questioned as if I were a wife in denial of my husband's ability to commit a crime. I was able to tell the reason why I knew he had not committed a crime. I felt the jurors' eyes burning through the side of my head, but I knew it only meant that they were paying close attention while I testified. I gained enough mental energy to look the jurors in the face with authority, and I gained even more energy from their cold stares at me while I was talking. I didn't have any fear. I felt like a giant over this situation.

After all the questioning, I was asked to step down from the witness stand. As I passed by, the district attorney smiled at me and said, "Thank you." I walked out with confidence. I felt a weight lifted off my body, my mind, and my soul. I felt free.

The defense rested.

The state rested.

Court was adjourned.

We went home feeling as if everything was over and we were free. That is when I remembered the saying, "Don't wait until the battle is over to shout. Shout now because you know in the end you are going to win."

Little did I know it was the truth!

On the morning of August 2, my husband got up early, went to my oldest daughter's room, and gave her instructions about what to do if he did not come back home. She agreed to do what he said, but then told him she would give him back his papers when he got home later that day. She was speaking the positive into existence.

This was the fifth day in court, the day the jury would hear closing arguments and then deliberate. This was the day my husband's future would be revealed.

I was feeling anxious but confident that everything was going to be all right. I was able to go inside the courtroom and hear the closing arguments.

Then our attorney made an award-winning argument about how my husband was innocent.

Once the jury was sent for deliberation, the district attorney gave the judge and our attorneys a copy of the instructions that he had given to the jury about false allegations.

We all waited in the waiting room. Yes, we were all nervous. At that point I was ready to give up, but I knew I had to stay strong for my children and for my husband.

And then, it happened.

After an hour and a half, the jury returned with the verdict. My heart began to pump cold blood through my veins as anxiety overwhelmed me. I wanted to go into the courtroom and hear the verdict, but fear grasped me and weakened my innermost being, the part that kept me sane.

My body began to weaken like a flower deprived of water. Given the sick feeling in my gut, it was to my advantage that the investigator had me go sit in the waiting room. It was almost as if she felt my pulse racing — as if she could read my mind.

While my son, daughters, and I waited for the verdict, we prayed. As we sat in dead silence, I noticed the uneasiness of my youngest daughter.

I could not quite read her true feelings, but I knew something was wrong. As I observed her, she stood and then bolted out of the room. Concerned, I asked the investigator to go find her and check on her. When the investigator came back, she informed me that she was fine. The investigator then went to sit in the courtroom to hear the verdict. I sat at the edge of my seat while my eldest daughter cried, "I know it is not guilty! I know it is not guilty!" A few minutes later, I noticed the doorknob turning, and my heart began to beat like never before. The investigator opened the door and said softly, "Not guilty."

My body became numb, and my eldest daughter lay across my lap, weeping. I felt an intense weight of pain lift off my shoulders. In the midst of my tears, I told the investigator to go and tell my youngest daughter the verdict.

I sat on the sofa weeping silently, but tears were not enough to express my feelings. It was a bittersweet moment for my family and me. It was not only a gain, but also a loss of a piece that had been pestering us for a long time without our knowing it. It just felt out of place to be in place. I was willing to learn to cope with this feeling for my family's benefit.

As I sat trying to comprehend and gather the broken pieces, there he was. He had walked out the door as a bound man,

and now he was coming through the door a free man. I could see in his eyes that he had been crying, but I was sure they were tears of joy.

As my youngest daughter entered the room and joined us, she had tears in her eyes. This time they were tears of joy. She went to the corner of the waiting room, looked at her dad, and just smiled.

Our attorney, bless his heart, walked into the room and began to cry as well. I started to cry again after seeing him cry.

I begin to call our entire circle of friends to let them know the outcome. I called Jenny, who screamed so loud, it made me laugh. I could hear her husband in the background saying, "I told you it was going to be not guilty."

I was dreading making one call, and that was to Mary Louise's husband. I knew she was too ill to talk. I called him and told him the outcome. He said, "Didn't I tell you it was going to be not guilty?" I asked him not to tell her the news because of the dream I had had about her death. He said, "I still believe God is going to heal her, but I have to tell her because she would want to know."

After all the emotional moments, we all sat in the waiting room for the last time, speechless.

Our co-attorney gave my husband a new court date, this time to discuss getting the not-guilty case expunged. That was to be a good court date.

For the past three years my husband had been obligated to the bonding company. I took him to the bonding company for the last time.

My family and I met our attorney, co-attorney, and the investigator for lunch at our favorite restaurant. We were still overwhelmed by the outcome of the trial. We shared our thoughts and were very thankful to God for bringing us through a very bad situation.

After arriving home, I had a changed feeling; it was indescribable. The atmosphere was so sweet. I could actually hear my kids' laughter. I noticed for the first time in almost three years that my husband sat on the sofa with the kids in the family room and watched a movie with them. I could already see the difference in my family and the freedom they could now experience.

The next day I called Mary Louise's husband to ask if he had told her the outcome of the trial. He said that he had and that Mary Louise had responded, "Thank the Lord. It's about time."

Mary Louise died August 15. Just like in my dream, I believe she was waiting for my husband to be free so she could be free.

As for me, I have fought a good emotional fight throughout this ordeal. Many times, I wanted to break—I mean, really break down—but I couldn't. Many times, I wanted to run away, but I couldn't.

Many people didn't know what we were going through, but because of the truth and my faithfulness, God didn't bring my family to open shame, and that is "The Other Side of the Story."

Afterword

I feel I have told my side of the story. I have peace. I have been waiting to share what I went through. When the situation began to get worse before it got better, I began to wonder whether telling my story would help people in similar situations. I began to keep a journal of the events and the dates that took place.

I wanted to share how I survived going to court every month, taking a vacation day off from work, not for trips of leisure but for trips to the courthouse. The expense of paying for parking and dealing with the imperfection of a man-made justice system is more than enough to fill a book.

I really became inspired to write this story when my children were taken from me. I wanted to share how I began to build my faith and my trust in God. We may feel that we have that faith and trust already, but can you pass the test?

Because of that, I am moving forward without looking back. Will the memory of each event be there? My answer is yes. They remind me to give God thanks every day.

I can now see the effect this really had on my marriage. Instead of causing us to go our separate ways, it pulled us closer and helped us appreciate each other more.

We went through five different attorneys, one of whom dropped out because we were unable to pay. Four different district attorneys thought they could win their case, but in the end the instruction given to the jury was to base their decision on false allegations.

This experience has made me a much stronger woman. It has helped me appreciate my family and given me an even greater reason to appreciate *life*.

I realize that God always had a purpose and a plan while we were going through our situation. I did not understand why these things were happening to us, but somewhere along the line, I came to the conclusion that they happened for a reason.

It is very important to never give up on God. Trials and tribulations will come, but it is necessary to endure to the end. It is normal to be in the valley of doubt, disbelief, and even depression. I experienced them all. Writing this book has been a journey for me. While writing, I laughed, but mostly I cried. It was good therapy, and it helped me through the process of healing my mind and my soul.

I am a total believer that when you allow your mind to think negative, it will be negative, but when you allow your mind to think positive, it will be positive.

I was blessed to have praying people, therapists, and a circle of friends. The song that got me through everything is titled "Haven't Forgot" by J. Shep. That song came just in time.

Everything that was taken, God has restored, and He is not finished yet. God has blessings in store for everyone who crossed our path. Remember to always pray, read the Bible, love your family, and keep God first in your lives.

I was having a hard time bringing closure to this book. There was something missing, and I just could not pinpoint the reason as to why it was hard for me to end the story.

I had to go to the criminal justice building one day in August 2014. As I entered the building, I had a different feeling. It wasn't a feeling of fear but of relief and near completeness. I got on the elevator to go to the fourth floor.

When I got off, I walked toward the district attorney who was from the last trial. I suddenly became weak, with a quick, cold

from the last trial. I suddenly became weak, with a quick, cold sweat across my forehead. He didn't notice me, but as I walked slowly behind him, I began to feel the process of closure. I did not feel the fear I felt during the trial. It was as if I could have tapped him on the shoulder to say, "Hey, do you remember me?" In other words, I felt bold and free of the justice system.

As I waited, I noticed that reflection in the window in front of me was the other district attorney from the first trial. She was walking toward me but turned to the right to go to the elevators. I thought to myself, *this is crazy to have seen both D.A.s on the same day, in the same place, and in the same hour.* I wondered why this could possibly be happening.

As I left the building, I began to breathe a little more easily and realized I had been waiting to exhale. It was a sigh of relief. Total relief. My journey was complete.

Now you have it: my side of the story. Shared with you in black and white.

This book is my story, my struggle, my fight, my win, my life.

The Other Side of the Story.

Works Cited

King James Version Bible

New International Version Bible

J. Shep & Standard. "Haven't Forgot." Faith and the Promise. Vault Recording, 2013, CD.

J. Shep & Standard. "Let's Go." Faith and the Promise. Vault Recording, 2013, CD.

J. Shep & Standard. "I Can Depend on You." Faith and the Promise. Vault Recording, 2013,CD.

Keawe, Genoa. "Lei Nani." 1929. By Charles Namahoe. Hana Hou! Vol. 1. Hula Records, 1991. CD.

http://www.whatchristianswanttoknow.com/

A Message from an Anonymous Editor

When you let me know your deadline, I decided to stop what I was doing and begin reading your book. I knew today was the only time I might have a few hours of uninterrupted time. Well... once I started, I simply couldn't stop! I had to finish all of it!!! What an amazing journey your family has been through. I had NO idea how intense and how long the struggle really was. What a strong woman (like your Mom) you are! You always kept your smile in my presence and never once let it show. "Wow" is all I can say.

Pride could have easily discouraged you from documenting your journey...especially because family was involved (which you handled skillfully without really revealing who the accusers were.) Kuddos for not being vindictive and being gracious instead. God sees and knows all. I am also proud of you for vindicating your courageous husband, who refused to take a plea deal to a lie. Thanks for writing about "Your side of the Story" so the truth could be told once and for all.

This is an important book that has the potential to help so much people who are struggling with their faith in the face of great adversity and trials...similar to yours. If people read it, and really apply the real-life Godly principles you share, it will help to build their faith. They too can experience the power to overcome every fiery trial and experience victory in their lives.

By the way, I did not find many typos. I think there were only 3 in the whole book. Good job proofing! I've attached a file documenting the ones I found for your review.

Thanks again for allowing me to preview this great

story. I will delete the manuscript you sent and look forward to purchasing my own copy your dynamic book!

You are some author Priscilla!!! I pray God opens many platforms, both religious and secular, for you to share this story of triumph through waiting and depending on God! You can really sing Andre Crouch's song "Through it all!"

I join you in saying "To God Be The Glory!!!"

Made in the USA
Middletown, DE
03 March 2022

62002052R00092